OXFORDSHIRE WALKS

OXFORD, THE DOWNS & THE THAMES VALLEY

Nick Moon

This book completes a series of two providing a comprehensive coverage of walks throughout the whole of Oxfordshire (except the Chiltern part already covered in 'Chiltern Walks : Oxfordshire and West Buckinghamshire' by the same author). The walks included vary in length from 1.7 to 11.8 miles, but the majority are in, or have options in, the 5- to 7-mile range popular for half-day walks, although suggestions of possible combinations of walks are given for those preferring a full day's walk.

Each walk text gives details of nearby places of interest and is accompanied by a specially drawn map of the route which also indicates local pubs and a skeleton road network.

The author, Nick Moon, has lived on the Oxfordshire border or regularly visited the county all his life and has, for over 25 years, been an active member of the Oxford Fieldpaths Society, which seeks to protect and improve the county's footpath and bridleway network. Thanks to the help and encouragement of the late Don Gresswell MBE, he was introduced to the writing of books of walks and has since written or contributed to a number of publications in this field.

O·F·S

OTHER PUBLICATIONS BY NICK MOON:

Oxfordshire Walks:

Oxfordshire Walks 1: Oxford, the Cotswolds and the Cherwell Valley new edition 1998

Oxfordshire Walks 2: Oxford, The Downs and the Thames Valley new edition 2002

Chiltern Walks Trilogy:

Chiltern Walks 1: Hertfordshire, Bedfordshire and North Buckinghamshire: Book Castle new edition 2001

Chiltern Walks 2: Buckinghamshire: Book Castle new edition 1997

Chiltern Walks 3: Oxfordshire and West Buckinghamshire: Book Castle new edition 2001

Family Walks:

Family Walks 1: Chilterns – South: Book Castle 1997

Family Walks 2: Chilterns – North: Book Castle 1998

The d'Arcy Dalton Way across the Oxfordshire Cotswolds and Thames Valley: Book Castle 1999

The Chiltern Way: Book Castle 2000

First published April 1995
New edition June 2002
By The Book Castle
12 Church Street, Dunstable, Bedfordshire

© Nick Moon, 2002

Computer Typeset by Keyword, Aldbury, Herts.
Printed in Great Britain by Antony Rowe Ltd., Chippenham, Wilts.

ISBN 1 903747 12 0

Cover photograph: Thames towpath near Abingdon Bridge (Walk 3).
© Nick Moon.

CONTENTS

Possible Longer Walks Produced by Combining Walks Described in the Book

Walks					Miles	Km
4 A	+	5			16.6	26.7
4 B	+	5			14.4	23.2
5	+	6			16.8	27.0
14 A	+	15 A			17.1	27.5
14 A(pt)+		15 A/C(pt)+	16 A (pt) (anti-clockwise)		13.6	21.9
14 A(pt)+		15 A (pt)	+	16 A (pt) (clockwise)	15.2	24.5
14 A	+	15 B			12.2	19.6
14 A	+	15 B	+	16 A	22.8	36.7
14 A	+	15 C			15.4	24.9
14 A(pt)+		15 C (pt)	+	16 A (pt) (clockwise)	13.6	21.9
14 A	+	16 A			19.2	30.8
14 A	+	16 B			16.6	26.7
14 B	+	15 A			13.7	22.0
14 B	+	15 B			8.8	14.2
14 B	+	15 C			12.1	19.4
14 B	+	15 C	+	16 A	22.1	35.6
15 A	+	16 A			17.6	28.3
15 C	+	16 A			15.2	24.6
19	+	20 A			14.4	23.2
19	+	20 B			11.0	17.7
19	+	20 C			13.0	21.0
21	+	22 A			17.1	27.5
21	+	22 (A–B)			13.2	21.3
23 A	+	24			17.7	28.4
23 C	+	24			15.9	25.6
26	+	27			16.9	27.2
27	+	28			18.8	30.3

N.B. The above combinations may vary in length depending on the starting point and linking routes used. The figures given here represent the shortest feasible routes using links indicated on the plans.

INTRODUCTION

This book completes a series of two published by the Book Castle in association with the Oxford Fieldpaths Society describing walks throughout most of Oxfordshire, excluding only the Chiltern area already covered by 'Chiltern Walks : Oxfordshire and West Buckinghamshire' by the same author. Apart from the Downs and Chilterns in the south of the county, much of Oxfordshire remains to be discovered by all but local walkers, although it has a great variety of attractive landscapes to offer and many of its villages represent real gems of vernacular architecture. The resultant lack of use of the paths together with past neglect by landowners and local authorities led to many paths becoming obstructed and overgrown, but, in recent years, many have been restored to use and thanks to the kind co-operation of the County Council's Countryside Service and Bridges Department the more serious problems encountered in the preparation of this book have been resolved.

This volume covers the southern half of Oxfordshire south of a line from Burford through Witney and Oxford to Thame, but excluding the Chiltern Hills. Although much of this area falls within the wide valleys of the Thames, the Ock and Thame and is therefore relatively flat, the proximity of the hills ensures that interesting views abound even in the flattest areas and any slight rise generally offers superb views across the surrounding countryside. The higher hills, however, such as the Oxford Hills and those around Faringdon provide commanding views across extensive swathes of the county while the relatively treeless and hedgeless sweep of the Downs with their steep slopes, lofty ridges and deep combes offer breathtaking scenery difficult to match anywhere in Southern England.

Apart from the Downs which form the book's southern boundary, the area can be divided broadly into four parts. To the north of the Thames and west of Oxford is the wide upper Thames Valley which rises gently from the river and the ingenious manmade landscape of dikes and drainage ditches of the Bampton Polderland to the first ridges of the Cotswolds along the Gloucestershire border and the ancient Oxford– Gloucester road where, on a clear day, the lowland to the south and east allows clear views right across the county to the Downs and distant Chilterns. Here the picturesque villages and small towns are built in the Cotswold style, with slate roofs giving way to thatch as one travels east.

To the south of the Thames is the broad valley of the River Ock better known as the Vale of the White Horse bounded to the south by the Downs and to the north and west by a generally low ridge known as the Corallian Hills which separates it from the upper Thames Valley and the Cole valley on the Wiltshire border. Here the fields are divided by a network of streams and the landscape is broken up by a scattering of copses and tree belts, while frequent views of the Downs contribute to its interest. The villages, which are again attractive, gradually change from stone to brick as one travels east and roofs are of thatch or tile.

5

In the centre of the county are the Oxford Hills through which the Thames wends its way from its upper valley into the wide plain to the southeast. Here ancient stone cottages have been supplemented by numerous more modern brick houses, but a greater proportion of trees and woodland than elsewhere in the county serves to disguise the level of development while a number of fine views across the 'City of Dreaming Spires' and the surrounding low-lying areas of the county reward the walker for his/her efforts.

Finally, to the east of the River Thame and north of the Thames is an area of gently undulating country sometimes referred to as the Oxfordshire Plain which separates these rivers from the lofty Chiltern escarpment. Here the last of the Cotswold stone cottages give way to the brick and flint of the Chilterns with frequent use of thatch and gentle climbs are rewarded by panoramic views towards the Chilterns and Downs. Despite the development pressure from the South-East which has brought the M40 and several golf courses, much of the countryside remains quiet and remote in comparison to the nearby Chilterns which are overrun with walkers at weekends and so this area provides an attractive alternative for those who prefer to walk in relatively empty countryside.

The majority of walks in this book are in, or have options in, the 5–7 miles range, which is justifiably popular for half-day walks, but, for the less energetic or for short winter afternoons, a few shorter versions are indicated in the text, while others can be devised with the help of a map. In addition, a number of walks in the 7–12 mile range are included for those preferring a leisurely day's walk or for longer spring and summer afternoons, while a list of possible combinations of walks is provided for those favouring a full day's walk of up to 22 miles.

Details of how to reach the starting points by car and where to park are given in the introductory information to each walk and any convenient railway stations are shown on the accompanying plan. As bus services are liable to frequent change, including information in this book might prove more misleading than helpful and so those wishing to reach the walk by bus are advised to obtain up-to-date information by telephoning the national hotline on 0870 608 2608.

All the walks described here follow public rights of way, use recognised permissive paths or cross public open space. As the majority of walks cross land used for economic purposes such as agriculture, forestry or the rearing of game, walkers are urged to follow the Country Code at all times:

- Guard against all risk of fire
- Fasten all gates
- Keep dogs under proper control
- Keep to the paths across farmland
- Avoid damaging fences, hedges and walls
- Leave no litter – take it home

- Safeguard water supplies
- Protect wild life, wild plants and trees
- Go carefully on country roads on the right-hand side facing oncoming traffic
- Respect the life of the countryside

Observing these rules helps prevent financial loss to landowners and damage to the environment, as well as the all-too-frequent bad feeling towards walkers in the countryside.

While it is hoped that the special maps provided with each walk will assist the user to complete the walks without going astray and skeleton details of the surrounding road network are given to enable walkers to shorten the routes in emergency, it is always advisable to take an Ordnance Survey map with you to enable you to shorten or otherwise vary the routes without using roads or get your bearings if you do become lost. Details of the appropriate maps are given in the introduction to each walk.

As for other equipment, readers are advised that some mud will normally be encountered on most walks particularly in woodland or shady green lanes except in the driest weather. However walking boots are to be recommended at all times, as, even when there are no mud problems, hard ruts or rough surfaces make the protection given by boots to the ankles desirable. In addition, as few Oxfordshire paths are heavily used, overgrowth is prevalent around stiles and hedge gaps particularly in summer. To avoid resultant discomfort to walkers, protective clothing is therefore always advisable.

In order to assist in co-ordinating the plans and the texts, all the numbers of paths used have been shown on the plans and incorporated into the texts. These numbers consist of the official County Council footpath number with prefix letters used to indicate the parish concerned. It is therefore most helpful to use these when reporting any path problems you may find, together, if possible, with the national grid reference for the precise location of the trouble spot, as, in this way, the problem can be identified on the ground with a minimum of time loss in looking for it. National grid references can, however, only be calculated with the help of Ordnance Survey Landranger, Explorer, Outdoor Leisure or Pathfinder maps and an explanation of how this is done can be found in the Key to all except Pathfinder maps.

The length of time required for any particular walk depends on a number of factors such as your personal walking speed, the number of hills, stiles, etc. to be negotiated, whether or not you stop to rest, eat or drink, investigate places of interest, etc. and the number of impediments such as mud, crops, overgrowth, ploughing, etc. you encounter, but generally an average speed of between two and two and a half miles per hour is about right. It is, however, always advisable to allow extra time if you are limited by the daylight or catching a particular bus or train home in order to avoid your walk developing into a race against the clock.

Should you have problems with any of the paths used on the walks or find that the description given is no longer correct, the author would be most grateful if you could let him have details (c/o The Book Castle), so that attempts can be made to rectify the problem or the text can be corrected at the next reprint. Nevertheless, the author hopes that you will not encounter any serious problems and have pleasure from following the walks.

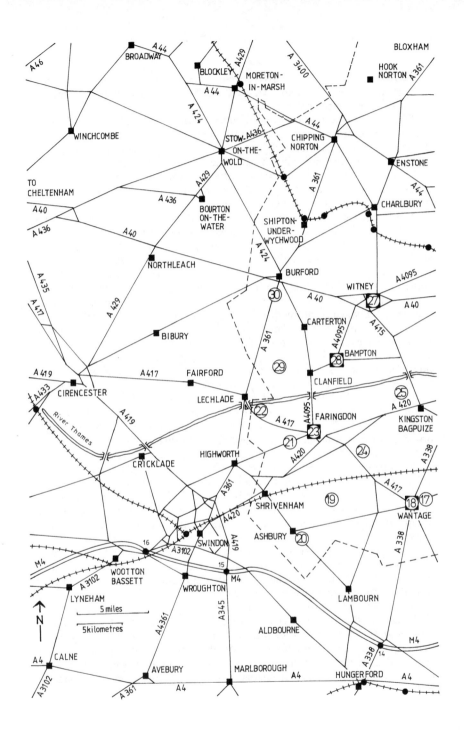

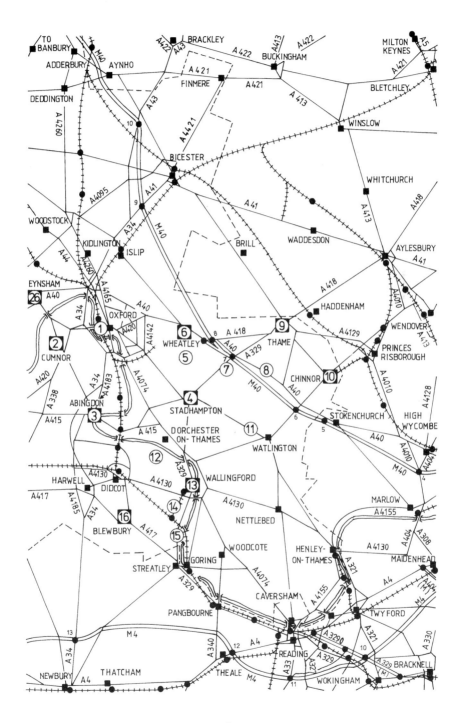

TO BANBURY
ADDERBURY
AYNHO
DEDDINGTON
BRACKLEY
BUCKINGHAM
MILTON KEYNES
FINMERE
BLETCHLEY
A421
A422
A422
A413
A422
A421
A421
A413
A421
A5
A43
M40
A43
A4421
A4421
A41
A41
WINSLOW
WHITCHURCH
WOODSTOCK
KIDLINGTON
ISLIP
BICESTER
BRILL
WADDESDON
AYLESBURY
A4095
A41
M40
A34
A44
A40
A418
A413
A418
A41
EYNSHAM
⌊26⌋ A40
OXFORD
WHEATLEY
⌊2⌋
CUMNOR
HADDENHAM
WENDOVER
PRINCES RISBOROUGH
A40
A40
A40
A40
A4142
⌊6⌋
⌊9⌋ A418
THAME
⌊5⌋
A329
A4129
A4010
A4013
A4128
A4010
1
⌊7⌋
⌊8⌋
CHINNOR
⌊10⌋
M40
A40
HIGH WYCOMBE
A420
A34
A338
A415
ABINGDON
⌊3⌋
STADHAMPTON
⌊4⌋
DORCHESTER ON-THAMES
⌊11⌋
WATLINGTON
STOKENCHURCH
A40
A4074
A34
A4183
A415
A420
⌊12⌋
A329
HARWELL
DIDCOT
⌊16⌋
BLEWBURY
⌊14⌋
⌊13⌋
WALLINGFORD
A4130
NETTLEBED
MARLOW
A4155
A4130
A417
A4185
A34
A417
A4130
A329
A4130
A404
A308
⌊15⌋
GORING
STREATLEY
WOODCOTE
HENLEY-ON-THAMES
MAIDENHEAD
A329
A4074
A4155
A321
A4
PANGBOURNE
CAVERSHAM
TWYFORD
A329
A321
A330
13
M4
NEWBURY
THATCHAM
THEALE
READING
WOKINGHAM
BRACKNELL
A34
A340
A4
A4
M4
A329
A33
A327
A329
A330
12
10
11

OXFORD FIELDPATHS SOCIETY

History

On the initiative of a number of people concerned about the increased use of the motor car on the footpaths in the countryside around Oxford, a meeting was held on 26th January 1926 'to form a Society for the preservation of Footpaths, Bridlepaths, and Commons in the neighbourhood of Oxford. Unless something is done to protect these, many of them will fall out of use and be forgotten. The ordinary road has more and more become either dangerous or disagreeable for the pedestrian, hence the preservation of the footpaths and bridlepaths is more necessary than ever. The latter are generally safer, quieter, and pleasanter than modern roads and brings one into much closer touch with the real country'.

The Society duly came into being, and over the years has worked constantly to protect and improve the network of public rights of way, not only in the countryside immediately around Oxford, but across the whole of the county of Oxfordshire. The Society today faces problems similar to those of 1926, but in many ways much more acute, as a result of the construction of new roads, industrial and housing developments and intensive farming.

What the Society does

Through its Executive Committee elected at the Annual General Meeting, the Society:

- makes representations to and co-operates with the appropriate local authorities on the maintenance, signposting and waymarking of rights of way
- submits claims with documentary evidence for additions to the Definitive Map of Rights of Way
- considers all proposals for alterations to rights of way, but resisting change unless there is significant public benefit
- co-operates with other amenity societies on the above matters
- owns tools which are available to members and other organisations for path clearance work
- arranges a programme of organised walks which is sent to all members. Walks are normally on Saturdays. The starting point of some walks can be reached by public transport.

Application for Membership to:
David Godfrey,
General Secretary,
23 Hawkswell House,
Hawkswell Gardens,
Oxford OX2 7EX

WALK 1:   OXFORD STATION

Length of Walk: 7.0 miles / 11.3 Km
Starting Point: Main entrance to Oxford Station.
Grid Ref: SP506062
Maps: OS Landranger Sheet 164
OS Explorer Sheet 180
OS Pathfinder Sheet 1116 (SP40/50)

Parking: There are various car parks at Oxford Station and elsewhere in the City Centre but, as these are expensive and approach roads tend to be congested, an alternative free car park on the walk route at North Hinksey may be preferable. For this take the A34 southwards from its junction with the A420 and after nearly a mile turn left onto a road signposted to North Hinksey where there is a small car park immediately on your right. (NB There is no access to this from the northbound carriageway of the A34.)

Notes: This walk should not be attempted when the River Thames is in flood.

Oxford, which the nineteenth-century poet Matthew Arnold dubbed as the 'City of Dreaming Spires' in his 'Scholar Gipsy', received this name not only because of its architectural beauty which attracts 1.5 million tourists every year but also because of its superb landscape setting. Indeed while the City has trebled in size since Matthew Arnold looked down on it from Boars Hill, a combination of the constraints of the river flood plains, the benevolence of some landowners and modern planning policies have ensured that areas of open country extend right to the heart of the City and so not only has the beauty of the views been preserved but numerous attractive walks remain possible from central Oxford.

Oxford Station, built on what was then the western edge of the City when the railway was extended northwards in about 1850, soon became the centre of a red-brick Victorian industrial suburb of factories and terraced cottages. In mediaeval times, however, the ancient parish of St. Thomas, in which it is located, was the

WALK 1

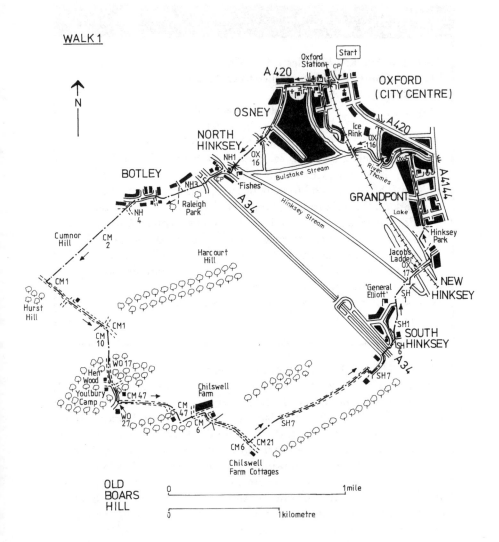

site of a number of fine religious buildings including Rewley Abbey, a Cistercian house founded by Edmund Earl of Cornwall in 1281 and the Augustinian Osney Abbey founded on Osney Island just west of the railway station by Robert d'Oilly in 1129. Osney Abbey had a massive, imposing church, an impression of which is preserved for posterity in glass in Christ Church Cathedral, but at the Reformation was suppressed and although it was at first intended to make the church into a cathedral, instead, like Rewley Abbey, it quickly fell victim to zealots who demolished it almost without trace, so that all that now remains of the mediaeval buildings is St. Thomas's Church, a twelfth-century structure largely rebuilt in the fifteenth century and a few fragments of stonework from the abbeys.

The walk soon leaves Oxford behind and takes you along the Monks' Causeway to North Hinksey before climbing to the heights of Cumnor Hill and the slopes of Boars Hill, where there are panoramic views across the County as well as the 'dreaming spires'. The return route then skirts the picturesque village of South Hinksey and sections of Oxford's riverside before reaching your starting point.

Starting from the main entrance to Oxford Station, turn right into Botley Road (A420) and follow it under the railway bridge, over the Thames (or Isis as it is known in Oxford) onto Osney Island where you pass the Church of St. Frideswide (the legendary founder of Oxford in 727AD). Having crossed another bridge, turn left into Ferry Hinksey Road (recalling the former name of North Hinksey) and follow it to its far end by the entrance to Kings Meadow.

Here take path OX16 straight on over a stile by a white gate and follow this fenced path to cross a bridge over Bulstake Stream. Now turn left then fork immediately right along a raised path called Monks' Causeway crossing another footbridge then continuing between hedges and eventually reaching a long floodwalk over a marshy area. At the far end of the floodwalk turn left to cross a bridge over Hinksey Stream at the site of the old ferry then take path NH1 straight on beside a right-hand wall to a gate into North Hinksey Lane by 'The Fishes' at North Hinksey.

Turn right onto this road then at a T-junction by the Norman church with a squat tower and ancient stone cross turn left passing a car park (**the alternative start**) and taking the left-hand footway to a crossing of the A34. (Alternatively use the A34 subway 250 yards to your right.) Cross this fast road with extreme care and go straight on to reach a side road. Turn right onto this then immediately left through the gates of Raleigh Park and take bridleway NH3 bearing slightly right onto a worn path leading uphill. After 250 yards ignore a branching path to your right and a crossing path then turn round for a fine view of 'the dreaming spires' of Oxford. Now continue uphill to two bridlegates then take the enclosed bridleway straight on to reach a right-angle bend in a road on the edge of Botley.

Here take Lime Road straight on passing Laburnum Road then at a slight right-hand bend by a bus stop fork left onto bridleway NH4 along a rough lane. At a three-way fork take the central option, a fenced path, straight on until you emerge by a stile into a field. Here take fenced bridleway CM2 straight on uphill beside a left-hand hedge soon with views to your right up the Cherwell valley and later over your right shoulder towards Beckley. On entering a second field, follow a right-hand fence straight on over Cumnor Hill soon with additional views over your left shoulder across Oxford towards Shotover Hill and the Chilterns and later to your right across Farmoor Reservoir towards the Cotswolds. At the far end of this field go through a hedge gap and turn left onto bridleway CM1. Take this fenced track straight on for nearly half a mile ignoring branching tracks to right and left by farm buildings and continuing to a crossing bridleway. 40 yards further on, fork right through a bridlegate onto bridleway CM10 crossing a field diagonally to enter Hen Wood. Now take bridleway WO17 straight on through the wood ignoring a stile to your right and soon entering an eroded sunken way.

On emerging at the end of a macadam road by Youlbury Scout Camp, former home of the noted archaeologist Sir Arthur Evans (1851–1941), take the road straight on. At a pronounced right-hand bend by an old oak tree turn left into a gravel lane (path WO27, soon CM47). Take this straight on to enter a field where fine views open out ahead across South Oxford towards Shotover Hill and the Chilterns and later to your left across the famous city skyline. Where the track turns right to the gate of Birch Copse House, go straight on leaving the track and following a right-hand fence downhill to cross a stile. Now turn right and follow a right-hand fence downhill to the bottom hedge then turn left and follow it to cross a stile onto a track near Chilswell Farm.

Here take bridleway CM6 straight on through a gate soon joining a concrete road and following it past some farm buildings. Just past a raised fuel tank turn right onto a branching concrete road which leaves the farm, becomes macadamed and bears left. Now ignore branching paths to right and left and take the farm road straight on over a rise. Near the bottom of the hill, 100 yards short of Chilswell Farm Cottages turn left through a bridlegate onto bridleway CM21 following a left-hand hedge to the far end of the field. Here go through a hedge gap then bear slightly right across a field to another hedge gap. Now take bridleway SH7 following a grassy track beside a right-hand hedge straight on through two fields soon with superb views across the city skyline to your left. At the far end of the second field follow the track bearing right into a short green lane then turn left onto a macadam road downhill soon bearing left to run parallel to the A34. By a garden centre turn right through a gap in the fence and cross the A34 with extreme care heading for the right-hand end of a crash-barrier on the far side of the southbound carriageway (or alternatively use the road bridge 650 yards further north). Now bear half left onto macadam path SH6 leading into South Hinksey then turn right into St. Lawrence Road.

At a left-hand bend near the thirteenth-century church with a fifteenth-century tower fork right into Barleycott Lane (SH6) soon bearing left. At the end of the lane turn left into John Pier's Lane (SH5) then almost immediately turn right over a stile onto path SH1 with Christ Church College and Cathedral coming into view ahead. Now head just left of Christ Church across a field which contained two llamas when walked in 1993 to cross a footbridge flanked by stiles by an electricity pole then turn left and follow a left-hand fence to a stile onto the end of Manor Road near the 'General Elliott'. Here take fenced macadam path SH1 called the Devil's Backbone straight on for 250 yards to cross a bridge over Hinksey Stream then take path OX17 soon climbing some steps to cross a long footbridge known as Jacob's Ladder over railway sidings and the London main line. Having crossed the railway, descend some steps to cross a bridge over a lake created by gravel extraction for construction of the railway to reach New Hinksey.

At the far side of the lake turn left through a kissing-gate into Hinksey Park and follow a gravel path along the shore of the lake to the far end of a smaller lake to your right. Here turn right onto a branching gravel path leading to a kissing-gate out of the park. Now turn left over a footbridge into Marlborough Road built on the site of the original railway terminus at Grandpont used from 1844 until the present station was opened. Take this road straight on for nearly half a mile then at its far end turn left onto the Thames towpath (OX4). After about 60 yards climb a ramp to cross a foot- and cycle-bridge over the river. At the far end of the bridge go straight on down the steps then at the bottom turn left then sharp right to take macadam path OX116 under the bridge. Now follow this path along the riverbank for 250 yards ignoring all branching paths to your right. On passing under an old railway bridge which formerly carried goods trains and gaspipes between the two parts of the old gasworks, turn left over a footbridge onto a path signposted to Botley Road and continue along the riverbank past the back of the Oxford Icerink. Having passed under a railway bridge carrying the main line, the path leaves the river and becomes fenced emerging through gates into a housing development. Here turn left passing some flats, crossing the end of a road and taking a macadam path straight on to rejoin the road. Now follow this road straight on into and along Mill Street to reach Botley Road (A420), onto which you turn right for your starting point.

Length of Walk: (A)   11.8 miles / 19.0 Km
                  (B)   5.0 miles / 8.1 Km
                  (C)   9.8 miles / 15.8 Km

Starting Point: Cumnor Village Hall.

Grid Ref: SP458045

Maps: OS Landranger Sheet 164
             OS Explorer Sheet 180
             OS Pathfinder Sheet 1116 (SP40/50)

How to get there / Parking: Cumnor, 3.5 miles southwest of Oxford, may be reached from the city by taking the A420 towards Swindon and Bristol to the top of Cumnor Hill. Here fork left onto the B4017. At the top of the slip road turn right then right again and then left onto the B4017 into Cumnor village. Take the B4017 straight on through the village for half a mile to reach the village hall on the left at the junction with Leys Road. Small parking areas are available on both sides of Leys Road where cars should be parked at right-angles to the road. If full, look for a suitable on-street parking space elsewhere in the village.

Notes: Walks A and B, in particular, should not be attempted when the River Thames is in flood.

Cumnor, on the hills west of Oxford made famous by the poet Matthew Arnold, also came to national attention in 1560 due to the mysterious death at Cumnor Place of Amy Robsart, wife of Lord Robert Dudley, the future Earl of Leicester and favourite of Elizabeth I. This mediaeval house built by Abingdon Abbey as a refuge for its monks was confiscated at the reformation and acquired in 1560 by Anthony Forster, an associate of Dudley's. During the Abingdon Fair of that year, when the house was virtually empty, Amy, who was staying there, was found dead at the foot of a staircase and to this day it has never been clarified whether her death was murder, suicide or an accident. As rumours were rife that Dudley was the Queen's lover, suspicions soon arose that Amy's death had been arranged and Sir Walter Scott

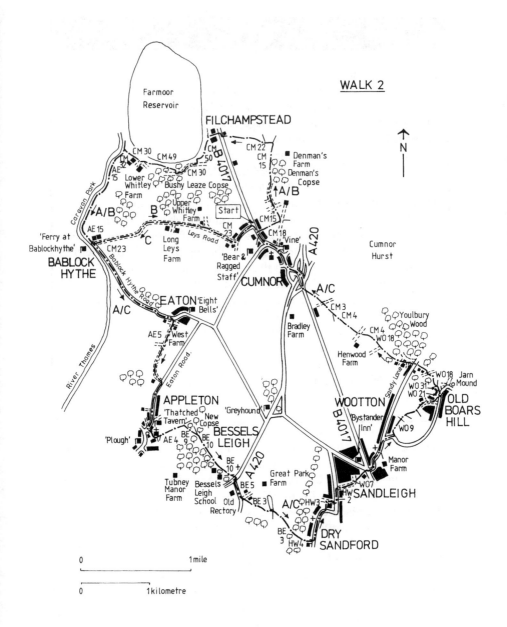

WALK 2

N

Farmoor Reservoir

FILCHAMPSTEAD

CM 30   CM 49   CM 50   CM 22
AE 15   CM 30
Lower Whitley Farm   Bushy Leaze Copse
Upper Whitley Farm   Start
CM 23
A/B   B
AE 15
C   Long Leys Farm

CM 15   Denman's Farm
CM   Denman's Copse
A/B

'Ferry at Bablockhythe'   CM 23

BABLOCK HYTHE

A/C   EATON 'Eight Bells'
AE 5   West Farm

CM 15
CM 18   'Vine'
A 420

'Bear & Ragged Staff'   CUMNOR   A/C   Cumnor Hurst

CM 3
CM 4
CM 4   Youlbury Wood
WO 18

Bradley Farm

Henwood Farm

River Thames   Eaton Road

Sandy Lane   WO 18   Jarn Mound
WO 31
WO 21   OLD BOARS HILL

APPLETON   'Greyhound'
'Thatched Tavern'   New Copse
'Plough'   AE 4   BE   BE
BESSELS LEIGH   WOOTTON
B 4017   'Bystander Inn'   WO 9

BE 10

Manor Farm

BE 10

Tubney Manor Farm   Bessels Leigh School   Old Rectory
BE 5   A 420   Great Park Farm
BE 3
A/C   HW 3   WO 7   HW   SANDLEIGH
2

BE 3   HW 4   DRY SANDFORD

0   1 mile

0   1 kilometre

18

embroidered this story in his 'Kenilworth', but nothing has ever been proved. This house at the rear of the twelfth-century church containing a statue of Elizabeth I and Anthony Forster's tomb, was finally demolished by the Earl of Abingdon in 1810 and its stones were used to rebuild Wytham Church.

All three walks lead you from the hilltop village of Cumnor with its mix of picturesque cottages and suburban sprawl down to Bablock Hythe on the Thames with fine views across the Thames valley. In addition, Walks A and B skirt the vast Farmoor Reservoir constructed in the 1960s and 1970s to provide water to Swindon and much of Oxfordshire and also used for watersports, while Walks A and C explore the quiet plateau country to the south around Eaton, Appleton and Bessels Leigh before passing through an outcrop of suburbia to reach Old Boars Hill, the one-time haunt of numerous poets including the former poets laureate Robert Bridges and John Masefield, with its fine views across the surrounding country.

Walks A and B start from Cumnor Village Halls and take the B4017 towards the village centre. After some 90 yards, turn left onto enclosed path CM18. On entering a field, follow a right-hand hedge straight on. Where the hedge bears right, leave it and continue to a signpost. Here do NOT join the farm road, but turn left onto path CM15 across the field to a gap left of a hedge of cypress trees. Now cross a metalled track and take a grassy track straight on left of the cypress hedge with magnificent views ahead across the Thames valley towards Wytham Hill and the Cotswolds, later with Farmoor Reservoir in the foreground. At the far end of the hedge the track bears slightly right and follows a left-hand fence downhill to gates. Now follow the edge of Denman's Copse, later a right-hand hedge downhill through two fields. At the bottom of the second field turn right through a gate, then sharp left, crossing a footbridge and stile and following a left-hand hedge. In the next field corner cross two stiles and a footbridge, then take path CM22 bearing slightly right across a field to a gate and stile in the far corner. Ignore a second gate to your right and follow a right-hand hedge to a gate and stile onto the B4017 at Filchampstead.

Turn right onto this road and after 75 yards, turn left onto path CM50 following Lower Whitley Road. At its far end cross a footbridge and stile, then bear half left and follow a right-hand fence through two fields, soon with wide views to your right across Farmoor Reservoir. At the far end of the second field go through a kissing-gate then after 25 yards turn left onto a fenced path to a kissing-gate onto a farm road (path CM30). Turn right onto this and follow it for a quarter mile into Bushy Leaze Copse. Here look out for a gate to your right. Turn right through a kissing-gate beside the gate and take an obvious woodland path (CM49) to a footbridge and kissing-gate. Now follow a right-hand fence straight on, soon with more views of the reservoir to your right then dropping to a kissing-gate and footbridge onto the road near Lower Whitley Farm. Turn right onto this road (rejoining path CM30) and where it turns left into the farm, go straight on through a kissing-gate and along a fenced path to a footbridge and kissing-gate. Now follow a right-hand fence straight on to the bank of the Thames. Here turn left onto its towpath (CM32) crossing a gated bridge and taking a fenced path to another gate. Now on path AE15, follow the riverbank through a long meadow for nearly a mile to a gate and stile onto a road at Bablock Hythe, the site of a Roman ford and ancient vehicular ferry only abandoned after the Second World War. Here **Walk A** takes the road straight on and omits the next two paragraphs.

Walk B also takes the road straight on to a right-hand bend then forks left onto bridleway CM23 ignoring a drive to your left and passing through gates into a green lane. Take this straight on uphill for half a mile. At the top of the hill you emerge into a field and bear half right between electric fences towards Long Leys Farm with views to your left across the Thames valley towards Wytham Hill and over your right shoulder up the valley. By the farm join its drive and follow it straight on to reach the end of Leys Road, along which you continue to your starting point.

Walk C starts from Cumnor Village Hall and takes Leys Road to its end and then continues along bridleway CM23. Where the road forks, take the drive to Long Leys Farm straight on for a third of a mile to the farm, with views to your right of Farmoor Reservoir and Wytham Hill and later to your left up the Thames valley. By the farm, where the drive turns left, leave it and take a grassy track between electric fences straight on, eventually entering a green lane and following it downhill for half a mile to some gates. Here go through a bridlegate to reach Bablock Hythe Road where the river is 80 yards to your right. Turn left onto this road to join Walk A.

Walks A and C now take this road gently uphill for a mile to Eaton. On entering the village, at a left-hand bend turn right onto path AE5, a stone track towards a barn. By the barn take the track straight on with a fine view to your right across the Thames valley. Now take a stone track straight on. Where the track forks, take a grassy track straight on with more fine views to your right, eventually bearing left to reach Eaton Road. Turn right onto this and follow it into Appleton passing the 'Thatched Tavern'.

Just past the post office to your right turn left into Church Road for the churchyard gates. With the ancient manor house to your right, parts of which date from the twelfth century, take path AE4 passing right of the late Norman church with a fifteenth-century tower then bearing left across the churchyard to a footbridge and stile. Now keep straight on across a meadow and over another footbridge then follow a right-hand fence to enter a fenced path to a footbridge into New Copse. After 15 yards fork right onto path BE9 (successfully claimed by the local Ramblers after the landowner had blocked it off) and follow its waymarked winding course. At the far side of the wood join path BE10 and follow it straight on along the inside edge of the wood to a gate and stile into Bessels Leigh Park. Here go straight on, passing just left of a stone shed and a massive oak tree, then ignoring a private stile to your right and joining a right-hand fence. At the top of a slight rise bear half left across the park, heading just right of a spreading cedar with views of Bessels Leigh's Norman church to your left to cross a stile by gates onto the drive of Bessels Leigh School. Built in the nineteenth century by the Lenthall family who held the manor till 1965, this house replaced one bought by William Lenthall, MP for Woodstock and Speaker of the House of Commons during the Long Parliament, who was renowned for his resistance to Charles I's attempt to arrest five rebellious MPs in 1640.

Turn left onto this drive to reach the A420. Cross this dual-carriageway and turn right onto its far verge, almost immediately turning left into Rowleigh Lane (BE5). Having passed the Old Rectory, at a right-hand bend turn left over a stile onto path BE3 and bear slightly right crossing a field diagonally to a stile at the right-hand end of a copse. Now cross a causeway beside a left-hand pond, then turn right onto a farm road, almost immediately forking left by the end of a fence across a field to the right-hand end of a hedge. Here go straight on across the next field to a stile into a copse some 40 yards left of the left-hand-most electricity pole in the field. In the copse bear half right ignoring a branching path to your left and soon crossing a stone footbridge then take the more obvious path HW4 to a stile into a corner of a field. Bear slightly right across the field to a gate by a stone shed right of a cottage, then take a track past the cottage to a road at Dry Sandford.

Turn left onto its footway soon passing the Victorian church. Where the footway ends, follow the road round a right-hand bend then turn left onto fenced path HW3. On reaching a road, turn right then at a T-junction turn left. Just before a left-hand bend turn right into Lansdowne Road (bridleway HW2). Where the road ends, take macadam bridleway WO7 straight on, passing the end of a road then following back garden fences past a recreation ground to a crossroads at Sandleigh.

Cross the B4017 (Cumnor Road) and take the Wootton and Old Boars Hill road opposite for a third of a mile passing Wootton's late mediaeval church. At a junction turn right onto the Old Boars Hill road. After 200 yards at a right-hand bend turn left over a stile onto path WO9 and bear left beside a left-hand hedge, soon bearing right and crossing a series of three wooden fences with superb views to your right across the Thames valley towards Didcot Power Station and the Chilterns and Downs beyond. Ignore the stile of a crossing path in the left-hand hedge and follow the hedge straight on crossing two further stiles. Now bear slightly right diverging from the hedge to a stile in the next fence then bear slightly left to cross the left-hand of two stiles in the far corner of the field. Here follow a right-hand hedge to a gate and stile into a green lane at Old Boars Hill.

Take this lane straight on uphill to a T-junction. Here turn right into a lane which soon becomes macadamed and starts climbing again. Just past a left-hand cottage with a brown gate called 'Farleigh', turn left onto path WO21, a narrow alleyway between cottages leading uphill to another road. Turn left onto this road then at a sharp right-hand bend fork left into a stone lane (WO31) and follow it uphill to a macadam road. Here turn left onto path WO18 through a kissing-gate right of white gateposts into Matthew Arnold Field, which featured in his 'Scholar Gipsy', where there is a fine view across the Thames valley. Now bear half right to reach a kissing-gate in the hollow. Do NOT go through this but turn right along the outside edge of the scrub over a rise. Cross a stile in the left-hand fence and take a winding path straight on through woodland. After about 50 yards at a crossways turn right onto a fenced path to reach the drive to a castellated Victorian house then take a fenced path straight on downhill and up again. On entering a field, follow its left-hand edge straight on to a stile into Sandy Lane.

Cross this road and take path WO18 beside a wooden fence opposite straight on alongside a fine avenue of lime trees. Where the fence ends, take an ill-defined path straight on through the bushes, soon becoming enclosed by fences and crossing a macadam drive. On entering open woodland, take an obvious path straight on to a footbridge and stile. Here bear slightly left across a field to cross two stiles and a footbridge then follow a left-hand hedge to cross further stiles and a footbridge at the far end of the field. Now take path CM4 following a left-hand hedge to a gate and stile into a green lane with views of Henwood Farm to your left. Cross this lane and a stile left of an electricity pole opposite then follow a right-hand hedge straight on through two fields with views of Cumnor Hurst to your right and the distant Downs to your left. At the far end of the second field cross two stiles then bear slightly left across the next field heading for a bend in the left-hand hedge just short of its far end. Here bear right onto path CM3 following the left-hand hedge then a fence. Just past a clump of bushes to your left, bear slightly left crossing a farm track and a field heading just right of a green road sign to cross a stile and footbridge and climb steps to reach the B4017. Cross this road, turn right onto its footway and follow it over the A420 bridge. Now fork left (still on the B4017) and follow it for half a mile through Cumnor village to your starting point.

WALK 3:   ABINGDON

Length of Walk: 7.7 miles / 12.4 Km
Starting Point: Abingdon Bridge.
Grid Ref: SU500968
Maps: OS Landranger Sheet 164
OS Explorer Sheet 170
OS Pathfinder Sheet 1136 (SU49/59)
Parking: There are public car parks off the A415 at the southeast
end of Abingdon Bridge.
Notes: This walk is prone to flooding after heavy rain.

Abingdon, once the county town of Berkshire (in which it remained till 1974), is a picturesque riverside town with a wealth of interesting buildings. Dominated for nearly 900 years by an abbey founded in 675 AD and second in importance in mediaeval England only to Glastonbury, Abingdon became rich as a centre of the wool trade in the fifteenth century when both its main churches were remodelled and St. Helen's was enlarged and given its fine spire. From this period also comes Long Alley, the oldest of several rows of almshouses, built in 1446. At the Reformation the abbey was suppressed in 1538 and much of it was destroyed, but some of its buildings survived including its fifteenth-century gateway, the Long Gallery, a part stone and part timber-framed building from about 1500 and the thirteenth-century Checker Hall which now houses the Unicorn Theatre. Among the town's many other fine buildings are County Hall in the Market Place, constructed by Christopher Kempster, a pupil of Sir Christopher Wren, in about 1680 and described by the notoriously critical Sir Nikolaus Pevsner as the 'grandest' of its type in England, and the Old Gaol near the bridge, built as a model prison in 1805, converted into a corn mill in 1867 and then into an arts centre in the early 1970s.

The walk, which is very easy in nature, first briefly takes you through Abingdon's fascinating centre before following the tree-lined River Ock through a surprisingly rural narrow corridor between houses to reach open country. Now turning south with fine views towards the Downs, you pass through Drayton to reach the beautiful, historic riverside village of Sutton Courtenay, then cross the Thames at the renowned beauty spot of Sutton Pools to skirt Culham and follow the towpath back to Abingdon.

Starting from Abingdon Bridge (also known as Burford Bridge), first constructed in 1416 but extensively rebuilt in 1927, take the A415 (Bridge Street) into the town centre. By the originally Norman St. Nicholas' Church and County Hall turn sharp left into Market Place becoming East St. Helen's Street. At its far end by a triangular road island and the thirteenth-century St. Helen's Church bear half right onto the Ock Valley Walk passing right of the churchyard to reach the end of a cul-de-sac road. Here take the Ock Valley Walk straight on across the road and a bridge over a weir. Now take a gravel path along elongated wooded islands in the River Ock for nearly half a mile crossing another bridge at one point. On reaching a bridge on a cycle track merging from your right, keep straight on, crossing another bridge and taking a macadam path to a squeeze-stile by padlocked gates onto the B4017.

Cross this and turn left along it. After 30 yards, turn right through a squeeze-stile onto a macadam cycle track following a left-hand hedge through two fields and ignoring a branching path to your left. At the far end of the second field turn right onto a gravel path to cross a concrete bridge then turn left and take a fenced path along the bank of the stream. On crossing a bridge over the main River Ock, turn left along its bank for a third of a mile to cross a large footbridge over the Ock and a small bridge. Now turn right onto Mill Road soon joining the bank of the former Wilts and Berks Canal to your left, completed in 1810 but closed in 1914 due to its inability to compete with the Great Western Railway. Where the macadam road ends by New Cut Mill, take a gravel track (A2) straight on, soon turning left over the old canal and climbing gently. Where the track bears right, fork left into a green lane to reach the top of the rise where wide views towards the Downs open out ahead. Here keep straight on (now on DY7) for a further half mile to the B4017 on the edge of Drayton.

Here turn right then immediately left into Sutton Wick Lane leading into Sutton Wick. Just past an attractive duckpond fork right onto path DY13, a lane which soon loses its surface. At the end of the lane continue through a gap in a wall and straight on across a green to the corner of a wooden fence then take a fenced path to a kissing-gate into

Henleys Lane. Turn left along this road becoming Church Lane. Just past house no. 30 turn left onto fenced path DY11. On entering allotments, turn right and follow their edge to a corner near the churchyard. Go straight on through a gate and along a macadam path past the thirteenth-century church with a fifteenth-century north aisle and tower, of which the greatest treasure is a rare fourteenth-century alabaster reredos saved from destruction by Puritan zealots by burial in the churchyard and only rediscovered in the last century.

In the churchyard turn left onto a crossing path passing through a gate. Where the gravel path turns left, leave it and follow the right-hand hedge straight on through another gate then along a fenced track. Where the right-hand hedge ends, turn right onto crossing bridleway DY9 to reach the B4016. Cross this and take fenced path DY21 straight on over a stile. On crossing a footbridge, continue soon crossing a stile and following a left-hand hedge to a kissing-gate onto a concrete road (bridleway DY1) known as Drayton East Way. Turn left onto this towards Didcot Power Station and follow it to the Milton road. Now take what soon becomes a green lane straight on for two-thirds of a mile passing the sites of a Saxon village and a Roman villa to your left and with occasional views towards Boars Hill also to your left.

On nearing Sutton Courtenay (now on bridleway SC26), you pass two bungalows to your right and round a left-hand bend then turn sharp left over a footbridge and stile onto path SC14 bearing right and following a right-hand stream and sporadic hedge through two fields to a stile and kissing-gate by a cream cottage. Continue past the cottage then turn right over a footbridge onto enclosed path SC13 ignoring a branching path to your left and eventually reaching High Street. Turn right onto this then left into Old Wallingford Way (byway SC23). After some 75 yards turn left into a gravel lane (SC10) and follow it to a T-junction by a stone wall. Here turn right onto a concrete road (bridleway SC3). By the entrance to Cross Tree Farm turn left into a green lane. On rounding a sharp right-hand bend, turn left into narrow enclosed path SC11 which leads you to a macadam road at Sutton Courtenay Green.

Sutton Courtenay, a settlement since Neolithic times with a Roman villa nearby, was given to Abingdon Abbey as a place of retreat for its monks as early as 687 AD. The present Abbey near the village green, which was built as a grange in about 1350, was confiscated at the Reformation and is now a school. In the twelfth century the manor was given by Henry II to the Courtenay family, from whom part of its name

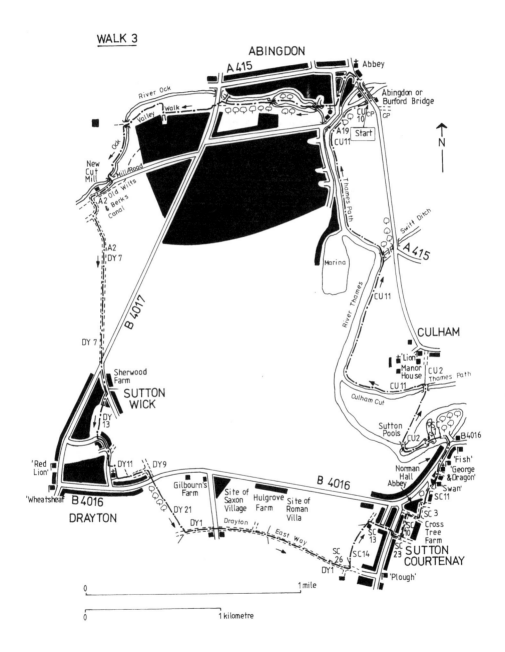

WALK 3

27

derives, and their original manor house known as Norman Hall dating from 1190 still stands almost opposite the twelfth-century church where Eric Blair (alias the author George Orwell) (1903–1950) and Herbert Henry Asquith, First Earl of Oxford and Prime Minister from 1908 to 1916, lie buried.

At the Green ignore a branching road to your right then at a fork keep right following a row of chestnut trees along the back of the Green past the 'Swan' and the church. By the 'George and Dragon' do NOT join the B4016 but bear slightly right onto a gravel path along the back of a narrow strip of green to join the road near a blind right-hand bend. Cross the road on the corner (where you can see both ways) and turn left onto path SC1, a gravel lane leading to Sutton Pools then take a clearly defined path (later CU2) over a series of footbridges and islands with numerous beautiful views of the river. On reaching the north bank, take a path bearing right to enter a field then follow a normally uncultivated path straight on across two fields to cross a large bridge over Culham Cut, constructed in 1809 to bypass the flash-weir under the old mill at Sutton Pools which was difficult for boats to negotiate.

At the far end of the bridge turn left onto the Thames Path (CU11), soon with a view to your right of Culham Church, rebuilt in the nineteenth century except for its eighteenth-century tower and the Manor House rebuilt by Thomas Bury in about 1610 on the site of another mediaeval grange of Abingdon Abbey. Now take the towpath for a mile along the banks of the Cut, later the old river. On reaching a fork, turn left over a long wooden bridge over Swift Ditch, the original course of the Thames until the monks of Abingdon Abbey diverted it in 1060 to supply the abbey and mill with water. In 1624 a lock was built to restore the river to its original course, but the construction of Abingdon Lock in 1790 made it revert to the monks' route and the original river has since become overgrown. To your right is a fine stone bridge built to carry the London–Abingdon road in about 1420 but abandoned in 1928 when the A415 was improved and a new bridge was constructed nearby. Now continue along the towpath for nearly another mile (later on path A19, then CU10) to reach a ramp up to the A415 at Abingdon Bridge.

Length of Walk:	(A) 8.0 miles / 12.9 Km
	(B) 5.8 miles / 9.4 Km
Starting Point:	Roundabout near Stadhampton Church at the junction of the A329 and B480.
Grid Ref:	SU604987
Maps:	OS Landranger Sheet 164
	OS Explorer Sheets 170 (both) & 171
	(or old Sheet 3) (Walk A only)
	OS Pathfinder Sheets 1136 (SU49/59) &
	1137 (SU69/79)

How to get there / Parking: Stadhampton, 7 miles southeast of Oxford, may be reached from the City by taking the B480 towards Watlington. In Stadhampton turn left onto the A329 towards Thame passing the 'Crown' then at the village green turn right into a side road along which you can park.

Notes: Parts of both walks are prone to flooding in wet weather.

Stadhampton, with its large village green at an important local crossroads, must once have been a place of strategic significance as it guarded the approach to the fifteenth-century Chiselhampton Bridge, once the only bridge over the River Thame between Wheatley and Dorchester. Indeed, in the Civil War in June 1643 it was as a result of Prince Rupert's concern that his Royalist forces might be ambushed at the bridge by the Earl of Essex that he took on the Parliamentarians at the Battle of Chalgrove Field and subsequently led his victorious army through Stadhampton on their way back to their headquarters in Oxford. It is questionable, however, whether the Royalists had local support as Stadhampton was the birthplace of John Owen, a friend of Oliver Cromwell who drew up a plan to reform the Church. Stadhampton's church is one which appears to have been much rebuilt over the centuries as parts of it date from the fourteenth and fifteenth centuries, while its Norman font suggests that it must be much older. The tower built in 1737 is notable for the four large stone urns at its corners, one of which was missing for many years before recently being replaced.

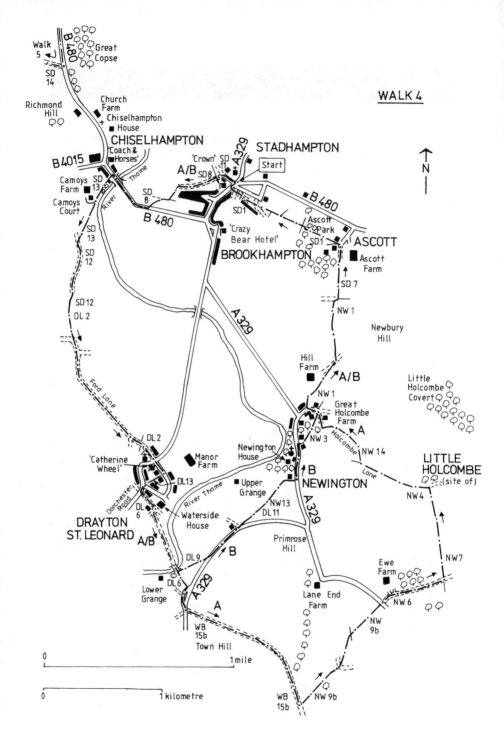

WALK 4

N

Both walks explore the Thame valley to the south of Stadhampton crossing Chiselhampton Bridge to visit the riverside villages of Chiselhampton and Drayton St. Leonard. Having recrossed the river, Walk B takes a direct route back through Newington while Walk A circles via Ewe Farm on a low ridge with superb views across the Thames valley and the lost village of Little Holcombe before both routes return via Ascott's seventeenth-century park to Stadhampton.

Both walks start from the roundabout near Stadhampton Church at the junction of the A329 and B480 and take the A329 towards the village for 30 yards then turn right into Copson Lane (path SD11) passing some cottages. After 130 yards at a slight right-hand bend turn left over a stile by a gate onto path SD8 and take a fenced grassy track to a gate and stile. Here bear half left across a small meadow to a corner of a fence then bear right along a narrow meadow. By a clump of bushes where the meadow widens, bear half left to cross a footbridge and stile then bear half right across a meadow to a stile onto the B480. Turn right onto its footway, with Chiselhampton House, a tall red-brick and stone manor house built for Charles Peers in 1768 soon coming into view ahead. Follow the B480 for a quarter-mile to Chiselhampton Bridge over the River Thame and the village which can boast a fine church built by Charles Peers in 1762 with its original box pews and gallery, a Jacobean pulpit and a painted bell and clock turret.

Having crossed the bridge, turn immediately left onto path SD13, the drive to a white cottage, leaving the drive and climbing steps right of the garage to a stile under a weeping willow. Now go straight on through a young plantation to a footbridge over the moat of Camoys Court. Here take an obvious path straight on along the bank of the Thame, passing a ring of tall poplars and Camoys Courts to your right, to cross a footbridge and reach a field. Now leave the riverbank bearing slightly right across the large field with views towards the Chiltern escarpment to your left and Richmond Hill over your right shoulder, to reach a hedge gap by a white marker-post and turn left onto a concrete road (SD12). After a quarter-mile, where the lane ends, go straight on over a culvert, then take a grassy track, bearing slightly right across a field to the end of a hedge. Now take DL2 (known as Ford Lane) beside this sporadic right-hand hedge. On reaching a bend in a farm road, follow it straight on with views to your left towards Newington's Georgian manor house and nearby church steeple and the Chiltern escarpment beyond, ignoring a branching farm road to your left. After two-thirds of a mile go through a gap by a gate on the edge of Drayton St. Leonard and keep left at a fork entering the village and passing its Norman church to your right to reach a crossroads by the 'Catherine Wheel'.

Here take Water Lane straight on. At a slight left-hand bend turn right into Gravel Walk (path DL13) between a hedge and a fence passing a bungalow and following its drive to a road junction by the war memorial. Here take Dorchester Road straight on. After 100 yards at the edge of the village turn left onto path DL6 along the drive to Waterside House. After 200 yards, just before a weatherboarded building with a steep tiled roof, turn right onto a concrete track, immediately bearing left onto a grassy track through a young plantation, then bearing slightly left and following first a left-hand, then a right-hand fence to a footbridge over the River Thame. At the far end of the footbridge **Walk A** takes path DL6 straight on across a field to a hedge gap leading to a layby on the A329. Now omit the next paragraph.

Walk B bears half left onto path DL9 crossing the field diagonally to a concealed gap in the far hedge level with the second mid-field electricity pole. Go through this gap then cross the A329 carefully and turn left along its verge. At a right-hand bend, just past a branching lane to your left, turn left over a stile onto path DL11 bearing half right across a field to cross a stile at the right-hand end of a wide gap in the next hedge. Now take path NW13 straight on over a slight rise to a gate in the far corner of the field. Go through this and bear half right through a young plantation, heading towards a tall poplar to cross two stiles and a footbridge onto the A329. Turn left onto its footway and follow it into Newington passing Newington House and Church (of Norman origin with a fifteenth-century tower and octagonal spire). Where the left-hand footway ends, cross the road then, at the far end of a parking bay, turn right through a green gate onto path NW3 soon entering a field. Here bear half left to cross a stile into a belt of trees where you drop down and cross a footbridge then keep straight on to a stile by an electricity pole right of a new house leading in a few yards to a farm road (path NW14) onto which you turn left rejoining Walk A. Now omit the next three paragraphs.

Walk A turns right into the layby. At its far end continue along the A329 for 50 yards then turn left though a hedge gap onto bridleway WB15b following a grassy track by a left-hand hedge and ditch for over three-quarters of a mile with views towards the Chilterns ahead. On entering a third field, continue for a further 160 yards then turn left over a sleeper bridge onto path NW9b bearing slightly left across a field to the left-hand end of a clump of trees surrounding a pond. Here go straight on towards a tree near the left-hand end of the next hedge to reach a bend in a grassy track. Now bear half left to the left-hand end of a wide gap in the hedge where you cross a culvert and bear slightly left uphill, with wide views to your right and behind of the Chilterns, Downs and Wittenham Clumps, to reach a hedge gap between a barn at Ewe Farm and a large oak tree. Here cross a road and take path NW6 straight on up a farm road past Ewe Farm. At the top of the hill where a left-hand plantation ends and you have panoramic views in virtually all directions, continue along the track for a further 250 yards ignoring a branching track to a model airstrip then parallel to the far end of a plantation some distance to your right turn left onto unmarked path NW7 heading just left of a twin-poled electricity pylon by the far hedge and passing right of the airstrip to reach a gap in the far hedge. Here bear slightly left down the next field to the near left-hand corner of a copse on the site of the lost hamlet of Little Holcombe.

Little Holcombe, which only ever seems to have been a small place, was apparently still a working farm in the early part of this century and its last ruined buildings only disappeared in about 1980. Holcombe Lane, the ancient road which gave access to it, was ploughed out in the early 1970s despite efforts by the amenity societies to save it and Dutch elm disease killed many of the trees which once lined it but the occasional midfield oak tree helps the keen observer to deduce its former course and extent.

Here turn left onto path NW4 (which follows the line of the ancient road) keeping left of a ditch and following it. Where the ditch ends, go straight on to a hedge gap and footbridge then keep straight on across the next field walking parallel to a left-hand hedge, which formed the southern boundary of the old road, to reach a footbridge in the far hedge. Do NOT cross this but turn right onto path NW14 (still on Holcombe Lane) following a left-hand hedge and ditch. At the far end of the field cross a stile and follow the left-hand hedge straight on, crossing a further stile then bearing right to a gate and rails into Great Holcombe Farm. Here take a farm road straight on, soon rejoining Walk B.

Walks A and B now follow the road bearing left and ignoring a branch to your right. Just past a left-hand barn turn right over a stile by gates onto path NW1 following a left-hand fence to a stile into a fenced path. Now cross a stile into a field and follow a right-hand hedge straight on with views to your left towards Didcot Power Station and the Downs. At the far end of the hedge turn right over a stile and bear half left across a paddock passing right of Hill Farm to reach a hunting-gate in the far corner. Now bear half right across the next field to a gate in the far hedge. Go through this gate then cross a rail-stile in the left-hand fence and follow the other side of this fence, later a hedge through three fields. At the far side of the third field, take path SD7 straight on through a hedge gap. Now follow a right-hand hedge to a stile and footbridge. Having crossed this, turn left over a stile by a gate and an old farm bridge and follow a right-hand stream straight on then continue across a field to a stile left of an oak tree into a marshy green lane. Take this lane gently uphill to join a track by some farm buildings. On reaching a macadam road, turn left through a gate into a farmyard and take path SD1 straight on over a stile by gates into Ascott Park which with its chapel, stone gateposts, avenues of lime trees, massive octagonal dovecote and extensive fishponds was laid out for Sir William Dormer, Sheriff of Oxfordshire, in 1660. Ascott House at its centre, however, was burnt down in 1662 before the Dormers could occupy it and was never rebuilt while its chapel was later demolished in about 1825.

Now follow a right-hand fence straight on through the park passing the dovecote and earthworks marking the site of the house to your left and continuing to the far end of the field. Here turn right over a fence then immediately left over a rail-stile into a belt of trees. Go straight on through the tree belt ignoring a crossing bridleway and continuing across a field, then beside a right-hand hedge to a stile in a field corner. Here keep straight on through wasteland then a copse of chestnut trees to reach a rough lane on the edge of Stadhampton Green. Turn right into this lane then where it bears right, leave it and go straight on across the green to join another track by some cottages. Where this turns right, take a macadam path straight on to reach the A329 near your starting point.

WALK 5:   CUDDESDON

Length of Walk: 7.5 miles / 12.1 Km
Starting Point: 'Bat and Ball', Cuddesdon.
Grid Ref: SP599029
Maps: OS Landranger Sheet 164
OS Explorer Sheets 170 & 180
OS Pathfinder Sheets 1116 (SP40/50) &
1136 (SU49/59)
How to get there / Parking: Cuddesdon, 6 miles southeast of
Oxford, may be reached from the City by taking the A40
towards London. Take the turning for Wheatley and Holton
and turn immediately right for Wheatley. At a mini-rounda-
bout go straight on downhill into Wheatley, keeping straight
on at two crossroads then taking Station Road/Ladder Hill
uphill out of the village. After 0.8 miles fork left onto the
Cuddesdon road. In Cuddesdon go straight on bearing right
at a junction then look for a parking space on the left near the
'Bat and Ball'.

Cuddesdon, one of the picturesque stone-built hilltop villages in
the Oxford Hills between Oxford and the Thame valley, is today
probably best-known for its Norman church which can be seen for
miles across the Thame valley and beyond and the theological
college built in 1854 for Bishop Wilberforce of Oxford by the young
Wantage-born architect George Street, who later went on to design
the Law Courts in London. The village, whose name means
'Cuthewine's Hill', is first recorded in a charter of 956 whereby the
king granted twenty hides of land to Abingdon Abbey. In 1634
Bishop Bancroft of Oxford built a palace here, the inauguration of
which was attended by Charles I, but in 1644 it was burnt down by
the retreating Royalists to prevent the Parliamentarians from using
it as a garrison.

The walk, which offers a succession of extensive views, explores
the fine hill country to the south and west of Cuddesdon first
dropping into the Thame valley to tiny Chippinghurst with its
ancient riverside manor house before crossing the hills to the

WALK 5

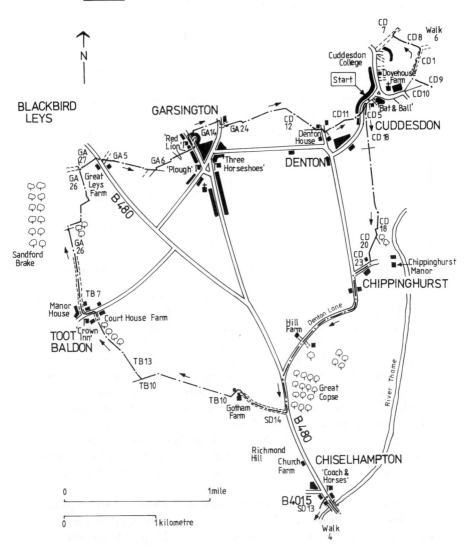

quaintly-named attractive hilltop village of Toot Baldon. You then descend into the Oxford basin passing close to the City boundary before climbing to Garsington and returning via Denton with another fine manor house in a secluded hollow to Cuddesdon.

Starting from the 'Bat and Ball' take Cuddesdon's High Street south-westwards. Just past the village hall turn left through gates into the recreation ground and take path CD5 bearing half right passing just left of some play equipment then heading for a thatched cottage. At the far corner of the field descend a bank but do NOT cross the stile. Instead bear half left over a footbridge onto path CD18 following a right-hand hedge downhill with fine views ahead towards the Chiltern escarpment. Where the hedge turns right, leave it and go straight on across a large field heading just right of Chippinghurst and a distant pylon to reach the far corner of the field where there is a fine view of Cuddesdon behind you. Here follow a right-hand stream straight on, ignoring the first culvert across it. Near the far end of the field where a hedge begins, turn right over a culvert then left and follow the left-hand hedge to cross a stile, footbridge and old stone stile. Now turn right to cross another stile then take path CD20 bearing half left across a field heading left of some farm cottages to cross a stile into a plantation leading to a footbridge. Here bear healf right through another plantation to cross a stile, then bear half left to a gate onto the Chippinghurst road (CD23), onto which you turn right.

At a T-junction turn left into Denton Lane and follow this quiet country road for nearly a mile over a hill with superb panoramic views of the surrounding countryside to reach a T-junction with the B480. Here turn left towards Stadhampton. After a quarter mile at a blind left-hand bend turn right onto path SD14, the rough road to Gotham Farm (pronounced 'Goat-hem') where there are fine views towards the Baldons ahead and Oxford, Shotover Hill and Garsington to your right. At the farm near the farmhouse leave the road passing right of a ruined building and taking a grassy track. By the far side of the farm garden bear half left across a derelict market garden to cross a stile and footbridge under a dead tree in the far corner. Now after 20 yards turn right through a hedge gap onto path TB10 and go straight across a field to a junction of hedges. Here go through a hedge gap crossing a culvert and follow a right-hand hedge uphill. At the top of the hill continue to a corner of the field then go through a hedge gap to your left and follow a left-hand hedge. Where the hedge turns left, turn right onto path TB13 heading for a terrace of yellowish cottages at Toot Baldon on the next ridge to reach a junction of hedges. Here cross a footbridge and stile and follow a right-hand ditch straight on uphill. At the far end of the field cross another footbridge and follow the fence of a right-hand tree-belt straight on uphill. By a barn at Court House Farm turn right over a rail-stile then left and take a lane past the farm, part of which is sixteenth-century, to the village street in Toot Baldon, onto which you turn left.

The name Toot Baldon is of Saxon origin, Baldon meaning 'Bealda's Hill' and also applying to three neighbouring settlements, while Toot means 'a look-out point' and is most appropriate when one sees how the land drops away into the Oxford basin. The village may, however, be even older as it is close to the line of the Roman road from Dorchester-on-Thames to Alchester near Bicester.

By the 'Crown Inn' turn right onto the road to the early seventeenth-century stone-built Manor House with its mullioned windows. Now take path TB7 straight on along a farm road with views of Cowley ahead and Garsington to your right, descending into the Oxford basin. Where the farm road ends, take path GA26 straight on across a field to a hedge gap just right of a distant gasholder and a pylon. Go through this then turn right and follow a right-hand hedge around two sides of the next field. Now continue through a hedge gap then turn right and follow a right-hand ditch to a field corner. Here turn left and follow a right-hand hedge. At the far end of the field, at the edge of a site recently saved from development as a football stadium, turn right through a bridlegate onto bridleway GA27 bearing slightly left to a bridlegate and stile left of a clump of trees. Here cross the B480 and turn right onto its footway.

Opposite Great Leys Farm ignore a bridleway to your left then just past a coniferous hedge turn left over a stile by a gate onto path GA5 crossing a field diagonally to a concealed stile in the far corner. Now bear half left across the next field heading for Garsington's prominent Norman church to cross a railway sleeper over a ditch then turn left and follow the ditch to another footbridge. Turn left over this onto path GA6 then turn immediately right and follow a right-hand hedge gradually bearing left. Where the hedge bears right, leave it and go straight on uphill to the corner of another hedge where there are fine views behind you towards the Downs and to your left across Oxford.

Now bear slightly right following the left-hand hedge uphill into an enclosed path leading to Oxford Road in Garsington, a stone-built village with ancient sunken lanes, a broken mediaeval cross and an Elizabethan manor house, much expanded by 1930's ribbon development and modern 'in-filling'.

Turn left onto the far pavement passing the 'Red Lion'. On reaching a fenced raised section, fork right onto a fenced path leading to a small gate onto path GA14. Take this raised path beside a stone wall to a rail-stile into a field then follow the right-hand hedge to a corner. Here bear slightly left across the field to cross a rail-stile on the ridgetop where there are fine views of the Chilterns ahead and across Oxford behind you. Now head for Cuddesdon Church on the next ridge to cross a stile leading to Wheatley Road.

Turn right onto its far pavement passing a cottage then turn left onto path GA24 down a rough lane. At the end of the lane go straight on over a stile and follow a right-hand hedge downhill through two fields. In the second field look out for and cross a stile in the right-hand hedge then continue along the other side of the hedge to a stile. Here bear slightly right across the next field towards cottages at Cuddesdon on the skyline to cross a sunken footbridge over a deep ditch in the next hedge. Now take path CD12 with a fine view of Cuddesdon College on a hilltop to your left, bearing half right across a field passing just left of an electricity pole to cross a stile. Here go straight on towards the fine early seventeenth-century Denton House to cross a stile in the far corner of the field noting a folly to your right in the form of a stone wall with a large gothic church window. Now follow a right-hand fence through a paddock and cottage garden to a road in Denton.

Turn right onto this road forking immediately left then left again over a footbridge and stile onto path CD11 heading for the upper group of cottages at Cuddesdon to a stile in the top hedge just right of a gate in the top left-hand corner of the field. Now follow a left-hand fence to a stile into a cottage garden then take a macadam path straight on past the cottage to the end of the village High Street in Cuddesdon leading straight on to your starting point.

WALK 6:   WHEATLEY

Length of Walk: 9.0 miles / 14.4 Km
Starting Point: Car park opposite Wheatley Church.
Grid Ref: SP597058
Maps: OS Landranger Sheet 164
OS Explorer Sheet 180
OS Pathfinder Sheets 1116 (SP40/50) &
1117 (SP60/70)
How to get there / Parking: Wheatley, 5 miles east of Oxford,
may be reached from the City by taking the A40 towards
London. Take the turning for Wheatley and Holton and turn
immediately right for Wheatley. At a mini-roundabout go
straight on down Holloway Road then turn left into Church
Road and look out for a car park on your right signposted
'Library'.

Wheatley, in a fold of the Oxford Hills south of the A40
London–Oxford road, is today a large commuter village not far
from the edge of Oxford, but historically it was an industrial
settlement with quarries dating from mediaeval times providing
stone for the construction of Windsor Castle and the Oxford
colleges and a nineteenth-century brickworks supplying the bricks
for building Oxford's Victorian suburbs. Until 1775 the main
London–Oxford turnpike road passed through Wheatley's narrow
High Street, but it was then diverted to bypass the village and the
difficult climb over Shotover Plain. By 1964, however, Wheatley
had expanded along and across what was now the A40 and so with
its dualling the village was again bypassed by the modern line of
the main road. Despite Wheatley's sprawl of modern development,
the old village centre is characterised by attractive cottages and
inns built of local stone or brick and is dominated by its fine
hillside church with a hexagonal spire by the celebrated Victorian
architect George Street. Street, who originated from Wantage, was
still relatively unknown when he was commissioned by Bishop
Samuel Wilberforce of Oxford to build this church, but the young
architect, whose studies of Continental Gothic church architecture

can be recognised in the French style of Wheatley Church, went on to design London's Law Courts.

The walk, though crossing a number of main roads, is one of considerable variety offering a series of spectacular views, passing the idyllic River Thame mills at Waterstock and Cuddesdon and visiting the interesting villages of Waterperry and Great Milton.

Starting from the car park entrance opposite Wheatley Church, turn right into Church Road and follow it to a T-junction with London Road, the pre-1964 line of the A40, by the 'Kings Arms'. Turn right onto this then immediately left into Old London Road, part of the turnpike road before it was straightened in the 1920s. After some 350 yards turn left onto the Holton road passing under the A40. Opposite the entrance to part of Oxford Brookes University with its 1960s tower-block set in former parkland, turn right over a stile by a gate onto path HO8 following a left-hand fence with fine views ahead towards the Chiltern escarpment and to your left towards Brill. Where the fence bears slightly right, fork left over a stile and head just left of the nearest pylon crossing another stile, then heading for the left-hand end of a line of tall poplars to reach a stile by some green stables. Now continue over a further stile and a single-pole gate to the Waterperry road by the drive to Holton Mill.

Turn right onto the Waterperry road and follow it over the M40. At the far end of the bridge turn right over a crash-barrier onto path WP11 descending a flight of steps, crossing a stile and turning right beside the M40 fence. After 75 yards bear half left through a young plantation to cross a rail-stile and sleeper-bridge under a willow tree. Here turn left beside a left-hand ditch to cross a footbridge and three stiles into the next field. Now go straight on to cross a stile midway between a dark brown wooden shed and a green barn at Waterperry and follow a left-hand garden fence to a stile onto the village street.

Waterperry is a cul-de-sac village best known today for the horticultural centre at Waterperry House. The gardens, Waterperry House (not open to the public) with its classical façade dating from 1713 and seventeenth-century wing and the parish church with its wooden tower can all be reached through gates at the end of the village street. The church is of Saxon origin but mainly dates from the thirteenth to fifteenth centuries. It can boast some rare grisaille glass from about 1220, a seventeenth-century three-decker pulpit and eighteenth-century box pews with brass candlesticks.

Turn right onto the village street. Just before it forks, by the end of a wall, turn right onto path WP10a following a left-hand hedge to a kissing-gate by a barn. Here take the fenced path straight on, then ignore a crossing drive and follow a left-hand ditch. Where the ditch bears left, follow it joining bridleway WP12, a gravel track and keep straight on, with fine views of Waterperry House to your left, to reach a gate. Here turn left onto fenced path WP12a with more fine views of Waterperry House. On reaching a drive, turn right onto it and follow it for nearly half a mile passing a thatched cottage, rejoining bridleway WP12 and eventually reaching Bow Bridge over the picturesque River Thame. Cross this and take bridleway WS2a straight on passing the timber-framed Waterstock Mill and following its drive to a road on the edge of Waterstock where you leave the Oxfordshire Way.

The tiny village of Waterstock to your left has an eighteenth-century manor house and a church restored by Street in 1858 with a fifteenth-century tower and a nave and chancel rebuilt in 1790. Inside is a bust of Sir George Croke, a seventeenth-century judge who defended John Hampden's refusal to pay Ship Money to Charles I during the build-up to the Civil War. In the past, Waterstock appears to have been a healthy place as between 1677 and 1785 it had only two rectors, Charles Hinde (1677–1726) and Edward Lewis (1726–1785), both of whom must have lived to a ripe old age!

Turn right onto this road and after about 140 yards turn right through a hedge gap onto path WS3 bearing half left across a golf course with views to your right towards Wheatley, heading for three tall poplar trees. At the far side of the course cross an overgrown stile and the A418. Now take path GM2 keeping right of a macadam drive and passing through a green gate into a field. Follow a left-hand hedge to a stile leading to the former Oxford–Thame railway line opened in 1864 and closed in 1963. Go straight on across the former railway to another stile into a field. Here follow a left-hand fence and sporadic hedge uphill to the M40 fence with more fine views to your right towards Wheatley. Now turn left over a stile and take a fenced path to cross a footbridge over the motorway. At the far end of the bridge cross a stile and follow a left-hand hedge to a hedge gap leading to the original line of the A40 (now a farm road).

Cross this former main road and go through a gap opposite, taking path GM2a over a high bridge over a spur of the M40 giving panoramic views of the surrounding countryside with the Chiltern escarpment to your left, the distant Downs ahead and the hills around Wheatley to your right. At the bottom of the steps turn left over a stile and follow a left-hand hedge to the far side of the field. Here cross a track and take a fenced path between a hedge and a plantation straight on turning right at one point and later left. Now ignore a crossing track then, where the fenced path turns right for a second time, leave it and go straight on over a squirrel fence and through the plantation. At the far side of the plantation cross a second squirrel fence and turn left onto a fenced path. Where an overgrown gate bars your way ahead, turn right over two stiles and take an old green lane known as Ives Gate Road straight on, crossing a stile at one point and continuing to a gate and stile on the edge of Great Milton. Here take a gravel drive straight on to reach the village green.

Great Milton, believed to be where the poet John Milton's ancestors originated and the source of his surname, is a picturesque village with a long narrow green flanked by thatched stone and brick cottages. The Norman church at the other end of the village restored by Sir George Gilbert Scott in 1850 contains monuments to the Dormer family including a relief of Sir Ambrose Dormer encamped at Calais and it is therefore somewhat ironic that their fifteenth-century manor house is now a noted French restaurant.

Turn right on to the village street and at the end of the village turn left over a stile by a gate onto path GM9 bearing half right across a field to cross a stile and footbridge in the bottom of a dip, then go through a kissing-gate. Now bear slightly left uphill to the top corner of the field. Here bear half left and follow a right-hand fence to cross a stile, then take a fenced path straight on uphill to a gate and stile onto a road opposite a barn at the top of a ridge where there are fine views behind you towards Great Milton and Brill. Turn right onto this road then at a junction turn left onto the Cuddesdon road and follow it for two-thirds of a mile descending with fine views across the Thame valley towards Cuddesdon with its prominent Norman church, crossing the River Thame at picturesque Cuddesdon Mill then climbing again.

About 150 yards beyond the mill, where the right-hand hedge ends, turn right over a stile onto path CD9 bearing half left across a field towards the right-hand end of a belt of trees on the skyline, with fine views to your left towards Wittenham Clumps and the Downs and to your right towards Brill, to pass through a hedge gap left of a junction of hedges. Now turn right to cross a stile then turn left and follow the left-hand hedge uphill ignoring a branching path to your left. On nearing Dovehouse Farm, cross the right-hand of two stiles then turn right onto a fenced cattle track (path CD1) and follow it with fine views ahead towards Brill and to your right towards the Chiltern escarpment. At the far end of this track turn left onto path CD8 following a left-hand fence to cross a stile at the far end of the field. Here turn right onto path CD7 following a grassy track downhill to a stile then continuing across a field to cross a stile and footbridge. Now take path WH6 bearing left beside a left-hand belt of trees. Where this tree-belt bears slightly left, turn right onto what is normally a crop break and follow it up Castle Hill.

Near the top of the hill, where traces of a Roman villa and Saxon burials have have been found suggesting that this was the original site of Wheatley and where there are panoramic views in almost every direction, turn left onto path WH5 following a farm track along the ridgetop. On nearing Castle Hill Farm, follow the track bearing right into a farmyard then keep straight on through the farmyard to join a macadam road which wends its way downhill into Wheatley. On reaching an estate road, turn left into Beech Road then right into Orchard Close. At its far end take path WH17 straight on to reach Crown Road, part of the pre-1775 turnpike road, by the house of the poet William Mickle who wrote 'The Ballad of Cumnor Hall'. Turn left onto this road then continue along High Street. By the Merry Bells Village Hall turn right into an alleyway then up some steps into the car park.

WALK 6

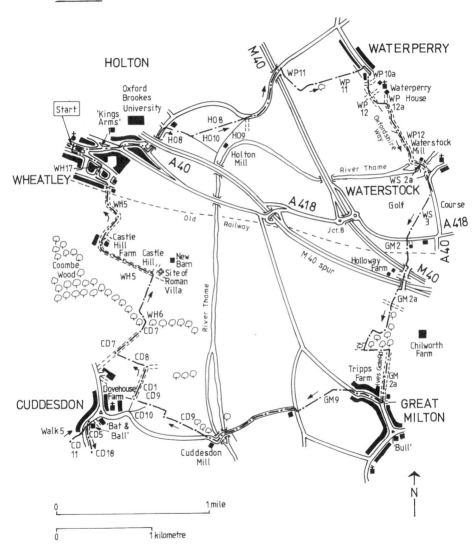

WALK 7: GREAT HASELEY

Length of Walk: (A) 8.6 miles / 13.9 Km
(B) 7.0 miles / 11.3 Km
(C) 3.3 miles / 5.3 Km

Starting Point: Gates of Great Haseley Churchyard.

Grid Ref: SP644017

Maps: OS Landranger Sheets 164 or 165
OS Explorer Sheets 171 (or old Sheet 3) & 180
OS Pathfinder Sheets 1117 (SP60/70) &
1137 (SU69/79)

How to get there / Parking: Great Haseley, 4.5 miles southwest
of Thame, may be reached from the town by taking the A329
towards Wallingford. Half a mile beyond the M40 turn left
onto a road signposted to Great Haseley. In the village ignore
a turning to the right then at a double bend turn left onto the
road signposted to Latchford. At a sharp right-hand bend fork
left into a rough cul-de-sac leading to the church where you
can park.

Notes: Stoney Lane (PY17) on Walks A and B may become
waterlogged and difficult to use in places in wet weather.

Great Haseley on a low ridge east of the Thame valley with its
thatched stone-built cottages and fine views across lowland
Oxfordshire towards the Chiltern escarpment may be considered as
the epitome of the English village. Apart from its picturesque
cottages Great Haseley has a fine tithe barn from about 1400 which
was once larger, a fourteenth-century former rectory rebuilt in 1846
and a seventeenth-century manor house. The substantial twelfth-
century church with a tower completed 300 years later, which is
prominent in the local landscape, has had several notable rectors
including John Leland, a sixteenth-century historian and Christopher
Wren, father of the architect and later Dean of Windsor, who was
expelled from the living by Cromwell's men. In the late 1980s Great
Haseley's beautiful setting was threatened by an horrendous proposal
to build a new town beside the M40 to the east of the village, but
thankfully, following a major public inquiry, this was rejected.

All three walks explore the quiet remote country to the southeast of Great Haseley with its lost or largely deserted villages and gently rolling landscape with fine views, while Walks A and C traverse part of the site saved from the developers by valiant local and national opposition.

All three walks start from the gates to Great Haseley churchyard and take path GH24 through the churchyard passing right of the church to a kissing-gate at the back of the churchyard where a fine view opens out ahead towards the Chilterns escarpment. Now go straight on, crossing a track, a stile and a small field to cross a second stile. Here **Walk C** bears slightly right across a second field to cross a stile in its right-hand fence. Now bear slightly right across the next field to a stile by an electricity pole into Latchford Lane. Turn left onto this road and follow it for two-thirds of a mile to its end by the gates to Latchford House. Now read the last but one paragraph.

Walks A and B turn right onto path GH25 aiming for the gable end of a red-brick cottage to pass through a fence gap left of an elderbush. Now continue across another field to a hedge gap leading to Latchford Lane opposite the red-brick cottage. Turn right onto this road, then immediately left onto bridleway GH5, the private road to Peggs Farm. At the farm keep straight on at first crossing a cattle grid then after a few yards turn right through a gate onto path GH26, a concrete track between farm buildings. Just past the farmhouse turn left through a gate into a field and bear half right heading towards the left-hand end of a plantation on the next rise to cross a stile then go straight on across the next field to cross two stiles and a footbridge. Now take path PY18 straight on uphill to a hedge gap just right of a taller section of the top hedge. Here cross a stile and turn right following a right-hand hedge then the edge of a plantation concealing the site of the lost village of Standhill.

Standhill, the bulk of which appears to have been located within the plantation and between it and Stoney Lane, is believed to have been a thriving village in the early Middle Ages with its own chapel first recorded in about 1180. In the fourteenth century, however, plague caused its depopulation and by 1600 the chapel is thought to have become disused. In 1745 its ruins were sketched and described by Thomas Delafield, rector of Great Haseley who said it was being used as a cowshed and was in danger of collapse. Today all that remains is a cottage on Stoney Lane and Standhill Farm and several cottages at nearby Lower Standhill.

After 40 yards, by a marker post, bear half right through the plantation, then across a field to a cottage rebuilt in the 1980s from a dilapidated ruin. By the cottage turn left onto Stoney Lane (PY17), the ancient spine road of Pyrton parish believed to be at least 1,200 years old. Take this straight on for nearly 2 miles with fine views in places ahead towards the hilltop hamlet of Clare and the Chilterns beyond and later to your left towards Poppets Hill and Stoke Talmage. Eventually the track enters a green lane which continues to the end of a macadam road by some cottages. Take this road straight on uphill for 250 yards. Having passing under a crossing powerline, turn left onto path PY20 up steps to a stile into a field. Here follow a right-hand fence straight on with fine views to your left towards the Oxford Hills and over your left shoulder towards Wittenham Clumps, Didcot Power Station and the Downs and later ahead towards Tetsworth and the Ashendon Hills and to your right towards the Chilterns. At the far end of the field cross a stile and follow a left-hand fence straight on through a field and past a barn to reach the road into Clare.

Clare, like Standhill, was a prosperous village in the early Middle Ages with 37 households recorded in 1279, but first the plague and then inclosure led to its depopulation so that there is now just a farm and a cluster of cottages, while to the north of Clare distinct outlines of old buildings can be perceived in a rough grass field.

Turn left onto this road and where it ends, turn right onto path PY13 passing left of a garage, taking a gravel path between two rows of cottages and crossing a lawn to a stile into a field with views towards Stoke Talmage ahead. Here go straight on towards North Farm. Having crossed a slight dip, bear half left down the field to a stile and footbridge just right of its bottom corner. Cross these and another stile then take path ST4 bearing half left across a field to a stile and footbridge in its far corner. Having cross these, cross another stile and follow a right-hand fence and sporadic hedge straight on to a field corner then turn left and follow a right-hand fence to the next corner. Now turn right over a stile and footbridge and follow a left-hand hedge through two paddocks to the village street in Stoke Talmage.

Stoke Talmage, in a sheltered hollow between Poppets Hill and Gilton Hill, was named after the noble Norman Talemasch family who were tenants of the manor in mediaeval times. The village, which has never been large, had a population of 140 in 1821 which has since declined to about 50. Its mediaeval church was so ruinous in 1758 that it had to be rebuilt and when 100 years later, the Hon. William Byron, cousin of the poet Lord Byron, became its rector, it was again in such poor condition that rebuilding was considered before Sir George Gilbert Scott was commissioned to restore it.

Turn left onto this road and where it ends, continue along a rough lane with views through the left-hand hedge towards Clare. Having crossed a cattle grid, turn right over a stile by a gate onto path ST5 following a right-hand hedge over Poppets Hill, with fine views to your left towards Wittenham Clumps, Didcot Power Station and the Downs and later ahead towards Great Haseley and the Oxford Hills. On crossing a stile onto a farm road, continue over a stile opposite then bear slightly right across a large field to the near left-hand corner of Cornwell Copse. Here bear slightly left along its outside edge to a corner of the field then turn left and follow a right-hand hedge. After some 30 yards turn right through a gate and go straight across the next field to a waymarked hedge gap leading into a plantation concealing the site of the former Cornwell Farm. In the plantation bear right onto path PY14 following its inside edge to a footbridge leading to a farm road. Cross this road, then turn left onto a path between hedges to another footbridge into a field. Now turn left and follow a left-hand ditch to the far side of the field. Here go straight on over a stile and footbridge then take path GH4a bearing slightly left across a field to a hedge gap and culvert. Now keep straight on across a field to the left-hand corner of a copse concealing a cottage destroyed by a bomb in World War II then bear half left across the field passing right of an electricity pole to cross a stile into Latchford Lane. Here **Walk B** turns left and takes this road for two-thirds of a mile then by an electricity pole to your right turn right over a concealed stile onto path GH24 and go straight across a field to a stile. Cross this and bear half left, aiming midway between Great Haseley Church and a black barn to cross a stile, then go straight on to cross a stile by a gate and a track. Here continue through a kissing-gate into the churchyard then retrace your steps to your starting point.

Walk A turns right onto the road rejoining **Walk C** and follows it to its end at Latchford by the gates to Latchford House. Here take bridleway GH3 straight on along the road to Latchford Farm. Where its macadam surface ends, fork left through a gate then fork left again onto path GH2 following the left-hand edge of a field past a stone building.

Now look out for stiles in the left-hand hedge. Turn left over these and bear slightly right across a meadow to a stile in the far fence. Here cross a footbridge and go straight on across two fields heading for the central of three large trees on the skyline to reach a stile and footbridge. Now keep straight on across the next field, with wide views towards the Chilterns to your right, to reach the far hedge then turn left and follow it for 350 yards to the site of an old farm.

Here go straight on to reach a farm road then bear half left to the far left-hand corner of the farm site. Now turn left onto path GH1 heading just right of an ash tree left of a hedge on the next rise to cross a stile and footbridge in the bottom hedge. Here turn left onto path GM17 following a left-hand hedge through three fields eventually passing Godwin's Copse and crossing a stile and L-shaped footbridge. Now bear slightly left onto path GH1 crossing the left-hand of two stiles, turning right and following the right-hand hedge. At the far end of the field turn left then immediately right onto a track beside a right-hand hedge. Some 40 yards short of the far end of the narrow field turn left across it to cross a culvert then follow a right-hand hedge uphill through a field and a recreation ground with wide views to your left towards the Chilterns. At the far side of the recreation ground follow the right-hand fence straight on to join a concrete track. By a scots pine tree turn right onto path GH24 through a kissing-gate into the churchyard. Now retrace your steps to your starting point.

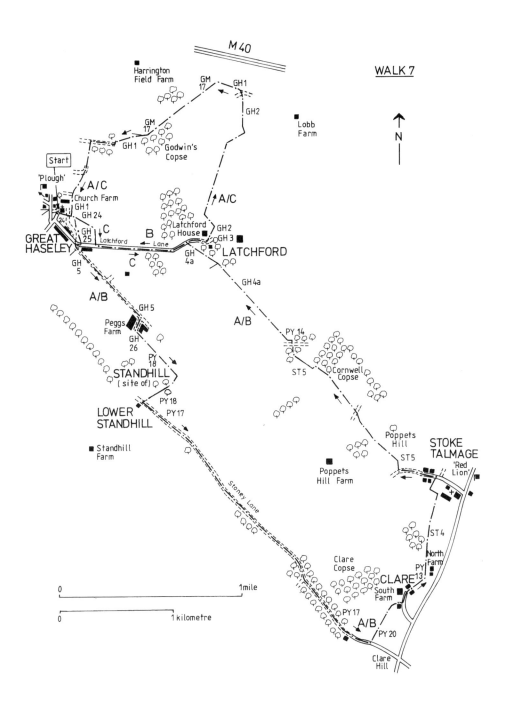

WALK 7

N

51

WALK 8: TETSWORTH

Length of Walk: 6.1 miles / 9.8 Km
Starting Point: Tetsworth War Memorial.
Grid Ref: SP687018
Maps: OS Landranger Sheet 165
OS Explorer Sheets 171 (or old Sheet 3) & 180
OS Pathfinder Sheets 1117 (SP60/70) &
1137 (SU69/79)
How to get there / Parking: Tetsworth, 3 miles southwest of
Thame, may be reached from the town by taking the A329
towards Wallingford for 3 miles to Milton Common then
turning left onto the A40 towards Stokenchurch. On reaching
Tetsworth village green, park on the right just past the bus
shelter or in the informal car park off Marsh End to your left.
Do NOT use the pub car park without the landlord's
permission.

Tetsworth with its spacious village green and cricketing tradition is perhaps the epitome of the English country village. Straddling the A40, the old London–Oxford turnpike road, Tetsworth was cut in half by heavy traffic until the M40 opened in 1974 and turned it into a sleepy rural backwater, but houses on the southern edge of the village now suffer from traffic noise from the motorway while the resultant loss of passing trade and a serious fire led to a lengthy closure of the 'Swan', the Elizabethan coaching inn at the eastern end of the green. In recent years, Tetsworth has successfully fought off two major threats in the form of a proposal to construct a massive new town 1 mile to the west in the fields between the village and Great Haseley and a large motorway service area also proposed for west of the village. During the construction of the M40, excavations revealed that in Norman times the village extended south of the ridge capped by the church, but either the exposed nature of this southwest-facing slope or the economic importance of the main road later caused it to move northwards.

The walk, which is generally easy in nature, explores the countryside to the east and south of Tetsworth characterised by its small or largely deserted hamlets and crosses several low hills with fine views, particularly towards the Chiltern escarpment. After passing through Adwell with its beautiful parkland, the walk joins the Oxfordshire Way and follows it back to Tetsworth.

Starting by Tetsworth War Memorial at the entrance to Back Street, take the A40 eastwards past the 'Swan' and up a rise. Just past the school turn left into Judd's Lane (bridleway TT67) climbing past Mount Hill Farm over a rise then descending gently, looking out for a stile in the right-hand hedge. Turn right over this onto path TT54 bearing slightly left across a field, with views of the Ashendon Hills in Buckinghamshire to your left, to reach a gate in a field corner. Here bear slightly right with fine views of the Chiltern escarpment opening out ahead, heading just left of the Stokenchurch telecom tower on the skyline to reach a stile into a small plantation. Now on path TT58, keep straight on through the plantation to enter a fenced grassy track between paddocks at Attington Stud. On reaching the second gate, turn left over a stile and take a fenced path to the back hedge then turn right and continue, eventually passing left of a barn. Now bear slightly right across a track to a stile by an electricity pole then take another fenced path between paddocks straight on, with fine views of the Chiltern escarpment ahead, crossing three further stiles to reach the B4012 at the scattered hamlet of Attington.

Turn right onto this road rounding a sharp left-hand bend. By a much-extended octagonal toll house, probably built when the road was turnpiked in 1770, turn left over a footbridge and stile onto path L1 beside a left-hand hedge at first then bearing slightly right to pass under a pylon. In the far corner of the field cross two stiles by gates and take path L3 beside a right-hand hedge to another gate and stile. Now bear slightly right across the next field to enter Upper Copcourt Farm by a gate and stile left of its largest barn. Here go straight on to cross a stile right of a weatherboarded barn onto the cul-de-sac road at Copcourt, a tiny hamlet straddling the ancient parish boundary of Lewknor and Aston Rowant, which must once have been situated at the top of the slight rise to the south of its present farms and cottages as its name means 'cottage on the hill'.

Turn left onto this road which soon becomes bridleway AR14. Where the road turns left towards the eighteenth-century moated manor, turn right onto a stony track. After 50 yards turn left onto a grassy track called Copcourt Church Way made in 1620 by order of the Bishop of Oxford to ease the journey of hamlet residents to the church in Aston Rowant. Follow this with fine views of the Ashendon Hills to your left and the Chilterns ahead and to your right, eventually dropping to a gate. Now take a grassy track by a right-hand hedge through two fields to a shallow ford then a fenced track to a gate. Here turn right over a stile onto path AR18 following a left-hand hedge to a stile into a plantation. At the far end of the plantation turn left over a stile into a field corner then turn right through a hedge gap into another field. Here follow a right-hand hedge, wiggling left at one point, to cross a footbridge and stile at the far end of the field. Now take path L5 by a right-hand fence straight on through two paddocks then bear half right across a third to cross two rail-stiles in the right-hand hedge. Here bear half left across two more paddocks to a rail-stile onto the drive to Blenheim Farm, onto which you turn left to reach a road in Postcombe.

Postcombe, though quite a large village which burial sites found on the line of the M40 show to have existed since at least the seventh century, has never been a separate parish and does not have a church. Until 1953 parts of the village were in the parish of Adwell as can be seen by the name Adwell Farm, but now the whole village is within Lewknor parish to which the bulk of Postcombe always belonged.

Turn left onto this road and at a junction take Box Tree Lane straight on past Adwell Farm to a T-junction with the A40 near the 'England's Rose'. Turn left onto its footway then right into Salt Lane, signposted to South Weston and Adwell. Having passed under the M40, turn right onto path L34 up a steep flight of steps to a stile. Now take a concrete road straight on beside the M40 for nearly half a mile past a hill called Adwell Cop to your left which is the subject of much local folklore. Having passed a telecommunications tower, continue (now on path AD1) to the far end of the next field then turn left over two stiles and follow a right-hand hedge downhill towards Adwell. At the bottom corner of the field ignore a hunting-gate ahead and turn right over a stile. Now follow the edge of a left-hand tree-belt to a hunting-gate onto a farm road, once the main access to Adwell village before it was severed by the M40. Turn left onto this road and follow it downhill through parkland into Adwell.

Adwell, with a population of 25 in 1981, must now be one of the smallest parishes in the country. The village itself would never seem to have been much bigger as the higher population figures before 1953 largely resulted from the houses in the parish in Postcombe.

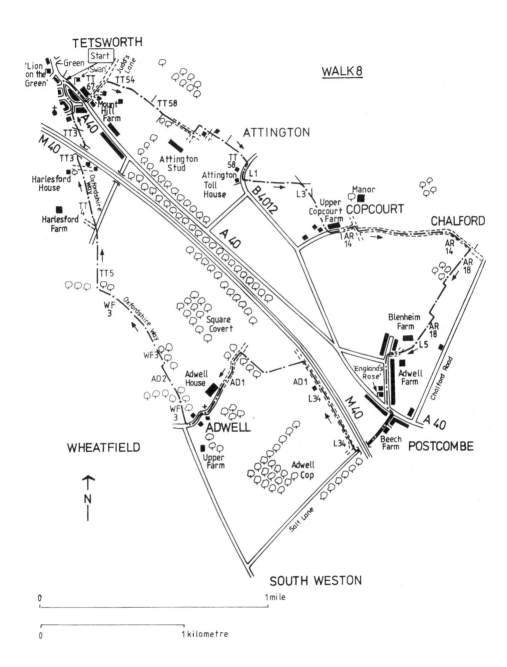

TETSWORTH

Start

WALK 8

'Lion on the Green'

Green

Swan

Judds Lane

TT 67

TT 54

TT 58

Mount Hill Farm

A40

M40

TT3

TT3

ATTINGTON

Harlesford House

Oxfordshire Way

Attington Stud

TT 58

Attington Toll House

L1

B4012

L3

Manor

COPCOURT

CHALFORD

Upper Copcourt Farm

AR 14

AR 14

TT4

Harlesford Farm

A 40

AR 18

TT5

Blenheim Farm

AR 18

WF 3

Oxfordshire Way

Square Covert

L5

WF3

AD2

Adwell House

AD1

AD1

'Englands Rose'

Adwell Farm

Chalford Road

A 40

WF 3

L34

M40

ADWELL

Upper Farm

L34

Beech Farm

POSTCOMBE

WHEATFIELD

Adwell Cop

N

Salt Lane

SOUTH WESTON

0   1 mile

0   1 kilometre

Adwell House, rebuilt in the eighteenth century, is noted for its Grecian staircase while the nearby church was rebuilt by Arthur Blomfield in 1865 after its twelfth-century predecessor was found to be too structurally weak to repair. The present church, however, retains the original doorway from the old church.

Continue along the village street past Adwell House and Church then uphill out of the village. Just before a road junction turn right over a stile by a gate onto path WF3 (part of the Oxfordshire Way) and follow a left-hand fence to a stile by a gate into a copse. Take an obvious path straight on through the copse to a stile then take path AD2 straight on across a field to cross a stile and footbridge right of a clump of bushes. Now turn right onto path WF3 following a right-hand hedge through two fields to cross a footbridge and stile into a third field. Bear slightly left across this field to a corner of a hedge where you turn right over a concealed stile. In a few yards cross a footbridge and stile under an ash tree then take path TT5 straight on across a field to a gate and stile in the far corner leading to a road. Turn right onto this road then immediately left over a footbridge and stile onto path TT4 crossing a field diagonally to cross a footbridge in the far corner. Now bear half right across two more fields to a stile onto a farm road. Cross this, go through a gap opposite and take path TT3 bearing slightly left across a field to a gate and stile leading to a tunnel under the M40. At the far end of the tunnel bear half left across a field heading just left of a red-roofed cottage at Tetsworth with uneven chimney pots to cross a stile. Now take a fenced path straight on to join a gravel drive by the cottage leading to a bend in a road then take Parkers Hill and Back Street straight on downhill to your starting point.

WALK 9:   THAME

Length of Walk:	8.9 miles / 14.3 Km
Starting Point:	Entrance from Priestend into Thame churchyard.
Grid Ref:	SP704064
Maps:	OS Landranger Sheet 165
	OS Explorer Sheet 180
	OS Pathfinder Sheet 1117 (SP60/70)

How to get there / Parking: From the centre of Thame take the High Street northwestwards going straight on at a mini-roundabout. At the far end of the High Street turn right into a cul-de-sac called Priestend and park near the church.

Notes: This walk should not be attempted when the River Thame is in flood. Path GH10 through the Old Paddock may be waterlogged and very muddy even in dry weather.

Thame, pronounced 'Tame', with its remarkably broad High Street, where the weekly livestock market used to be held and street markets and the annual fair take place to this day, despite a doubling of its population in recent years, remains the epitome of an English market town. Although the High Street with its attractive mixture of architectural styles dating from the fifteenth century to the present day particularly notable for some fine Georgian houses suggests haphazard development, it, in fact, results from a planned expansion of the town by the Bishop of Lincoln in the twelfth century which led to the establishment of a market in about 1184 and the diversion of the Aylesbury main road through the High Street in 1219. For this reason, for centuries the town centre was referred to as New Thame whereas the original village around the church was known as Old Thame. The present imposing church dates from the thirteenth century, but was later enlarged and had its tower heightened in the fifteenth century. Also from the thirteenth century is the nearby Prebendal House in Priestend, while the fine timber-framed brick tithe barn, the stone-built grammar school attended by the young John Hampden and the picturesque timber-framed almshouses all in Church Road

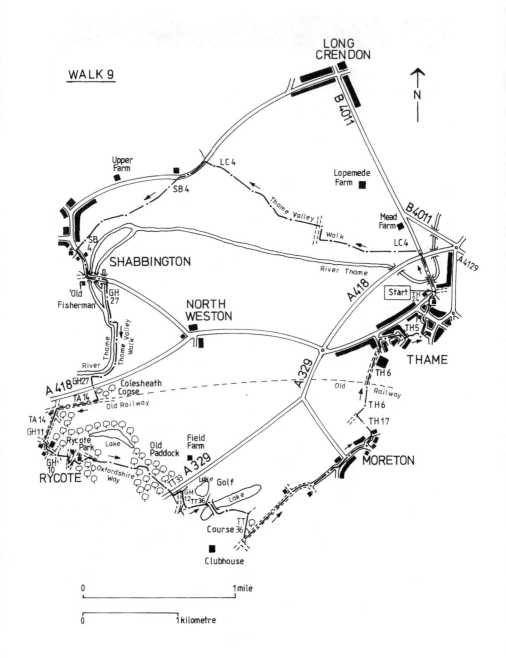

WALK 9

LONG CRENDON

N

B 4011

Upper Farm

LC 4

Lopemede Farm

SB 4

Thame Valley

Mead Farm

B 4011

SB 4

Walk

LC 4

A 4129

SHABBINGTON

River Thame

A 418

'Old Fisherman'

GH 27

NORTH WESTON

Start

TH 24

THE 5

River Thame

Thame Valley Walk

THAME

A 418 GH27

Coleusheath Copse

Old Railway

A 329

Old

Railway

TH 6

TA 14

Old Railway

TH 6

TA 14 GH11

TH 17

Rycote Park

Lake

Old Paddock

Field Farm

GH 10

Oxfordshire Way

A 329

MORETON

RYCOTE

TT 33

Lake

Golf

GH 12

TT 36

Lake

TT 36

Course

Clubhouse

0   1 mile

0   1 kilometre

58

date from the sixteenth century. In the Civil War the town came to national prominence when the Parliamentary forces used it as their headquarters in their struggle to take the Royalist stronghold of Oxford and it was here that in 1643 the local hero, John Hampden died as a result of a wound received at the Battle of Chalgrove Field. Perhaps Thame's greatest claim to fame today, however, is the annual agricultural show, which, together with the Fair, takes place on the third Thursday in September and is claimed to be the largest one-day show in England.

The walk, which is of an easy nature, immediately leaves Thame behind and explores the Thame valley west of the town first visiting the Buckinghamshire village of Shabbington with its thatched cottages and picturesque riverside inn before turning south to historic Rycote where several Tudor and Stuart monarchs stayed. Your return route then leads you by way of the Oxfordshire Golf Club with its large lake and Moreton, finally passing some of Thame's most historic buildings on your way back to the church.

Starting from the Priestend entrance to Thame churchyard, continue along Priestend passing a gate and taking a disused section of the old Bicester road straight on over Thame Bridge into Buckinghamshire to a fence gap onto the A418 Thame Bypass. Cross this road and go through a gap opposite onto another disused road. After some 60 yards turn left over a stile by gates onto path LC4 joining the Thame Valley Walk. Now follow a right-hand hedge, then a fence through two fields. At the far end of the second field cross two stiles and a footbridge and follow a left-hand fence to a field corner then turn right and follow a left-hand fence until you reach a stile in it onto a fenced track. Cross this and a stile opposite and go straight on across three fields to the right-hand end of a hedge. Here bear half right across the field to a corner of another hedge with views towards the hilltop village of Brill ahead, Long Crendon on a ridge to your right and Thame and Moreton backed by the Chilterns behind you. Now bear half left and follow a left-hand hedge straight on through four fields with Shabbington coming into view to your left in the fourth field to reach a gate and stile onto the Long Crendon– Shabbington road.

Turn left onto this road and follow it for some 350 yards to a long right-hand bend. Halfway round the bend turn left through a gate onto path SB4 bearing half right across a field with pronounced ridges and furrows denoting mediaeval strip cultivation and heading for an electricity pole left of Shabbington Church to cross a footbridge and stile in the far hedge. Now turn right and follow a right-hand hedge. Where the hedge bears right, leave it and bear slightly left across the field to cross a stile and footbridge in the far corner. Now follow a winding left-hand hedge with views of the River Thame to your left. Where the hedge turns sharp left, leave it and go straight on, joining another left-hand hedge and following it to a stile into a paddock. Follow the left-hand hedge straight on through the paddock to cross two stiles and a footbridge then bear slightly right towards Shabbington Church to reach a stile onto Ickford Road.

In mediaeval times Shabbington must have been a place of some importance as it had an abbey, of which only earthworks now remain, and a brick and stone church as early as the eleventh century. The nave of this church with its herringbone brickwork still survives but now has a fourteenth-century chancel and fifteenth-century tower.

Cross the road, turn left onto its footway and follow it downhill to the picturesque riverside 'Old Fisherman'. Here cross the road and take a raised flood walk beside the road, crossing bridges over both main arms and a backwater of the River Thame where the floodwalk ends. Now back in Oxfordshire, having crossed the third bridge, turn right over a footbridge and stile onto path GH27 following the riverbank for three-quarters of a mile through three fields. Where an unbridged ditch blocks your way ahead, turn left and follow it to a hedge gap onto the A418. Cross this road (and the ditch) and take path TA14 through a gap right of a bridge parapet opposite following the ditch along the edge of Colesheath Copse. At the far side of the field climb steps up the embankment of the former Thame–Oxford railway (opened in 1864 and closed in 1963) then turn right onto a grassy track on the old railway line. After a quarter-mile at a former level crossing near a cottage, turn left onto a crossing farm road and follow it gently uphill towards Home Farm (later on path GH11).

At a junction of tracks near a white cottage where the Thame Valley Walk meets the Oxfordshire Way, bear half left onto the Oxfordshire Way (path GH10) passing left of the cottage and swinging left behind farm buildings. Now go straight on across a farmyard and past a line of poplars then ignore a gate to the left and immediately bear slightly left across a field to cross a stile left of an electricity pole. Here continue to a second stile onto a stony drive where Rycote Park house comes into view to your left. Built in 1539 by Lord Williams, founder of the Thame grammar school, Rycote Park was originally a large moated red-brick house built round a courtyard which was visited on at least six occasions by four separate monarchs up to 1644. After Williams' death in 1559 Rycote passed to his son-in-law Sir Henry Norris whose descendants became the Earls of Abingdon from 1682. In 1745, however, much of the house was destroyed by fire and the Earl's son was killed with the result that his grief-stricken parents moved to Wytham and the house was not rebuilt until 1920 when the surviving stables and turret were converted into the house we see today.

Turn right onto this drive. Almost immediately turn sharp left onto a drive towards Rycote Chapel, soon turning right up some steps and taking a gravel path passing right of the chapel to reach an information kiosk. This chapel built by Sir Richard Quatremains in 1449 is interesting as it has survived virtually unaltered and contains a lavish Royal Pew built for Charles I's visit in 1625. Now pass right of the kiosk and take a winding path through a copse. On reaching a crossing track where there is a fine view of the house to your left, turn right onto it crossing the copse to enter a field by the corner of a fence. Here go straight on across a large parkland field to a waymarked path into the middle of a wood called Old Paddock. Take this path bearing left at first to cross a culvert then bearing right and following an obvious, if often muddy and waterlogged course through the wood to reach the A329.

Cross this and a stile opposite then turn left leaving the Oxfordshire Way and taking path TT33 behind the roadside hedge to a kissing-gate leading to the vehicular entrance to the Oxfordshire Golf Club. Cross this entrance, go through a kissing-gate opposite and take path GH12 between a brick wall and a ditch then bear right onto path TT36 and follow the bottom of mounding parallel to the gold course drive. By a second waymarking post where the drive begins to bear left, turn left over the mounding heading towards the clubhouse and passing left of two tees to reach a wide macadam path. Turn left onto this and follow it for some 300 yards with views across a small lake to your left towards Long Crendon and Brill. Ignore one branching path to your right then fork right onto a second leading to a long footbridge over a larger lake. Cross this bridge then bear slightly right towards an old oak tree. On reaching a waymarking post, turn left joining a macadam path along the shore of the lake at first then bearing right to reach a T-junction. Here turn right soon passing a clump of old oak trees. At a left-hand bend leave the macadam path and follow the waymarks straight on, crossing another macadam path and a stile to reach a junction of lanes. Here turn left into a gravel lane and follow it for over half a mile eventually bearing right by a farm to reach a bend in a macadam road. Bear left onto this and follow it into Moreton with views towards Thame ahead and the Chilterns to your right.

At a T-junction turn left then at a fork by the war memorial keep straight on. At another fork by a small village green with a seat and a pond go left. Where the road ends, bear slightly left onto enclosed path TH17 passing left of the entrance to Brook Cottage and right of a pond to cross a stile into a field. Now bear left across the field to cross a stile and footbridge in the far left-hand corner leading into a green lane. Here turn right onto path TH6 soon crossing some wooden rails and following the right-hand hedge straight on to a gate onto the course of the old railway. Cross this and take a green lane straight on for a quarter mile past the modern Lord Williams' School to reach Sycamore Drive on the edge of Thame.

Turn left onto its far pavement then turn right into Beech Road ignoring Chestnut Avenue to your right and eventually bearing right to reach the junction with Hazel Avenue. Here turn left onto path TH5 down a macadam alley soon crossing a bridge over Cuttle Brook. Now the path climbs and bears right then left. At a fork bear slightly left into Brook Lane, soon crossing the end of Mitchell Close. The lane then narrows and bears left then right to emerge into the High Street by the 'Six Bells'. Here cross the High Street and take Church Road left of a picturesque sixteenth-century cottage straight on, passing 'Booker Tate' (the original Lord Williams' Grammar School) to your right and the timber-framed sixteenth-century tithe barn with herringbone brickwork to your left. Now go straight on through gates into the churchyard and take path TH24 passing left of the church to reach a gate and steps in the back wall of the churchyard leading down to your starting point.

WALK 10: CHINNOR

Length of Walk: (A) 8.6 miles / 13.9 Km
(B) 6.1 miles / 9.9 Km
(C) 4.8 miles / 7.7 Km
Starting Point: Junction of High Street and Church Road, Chinnor.
Grid Ref: SP758010
Maps: OS Landranger Sheet 165
OS Explorer Sheet 181 (or old Sheet 2)
OS Pathfinder Sheet 1117 (SP60/70)

How to get there / Parking: Chinnor, 4.5 miles southeast of Thame, may be reached from the town by taking the B4445. On entering the village, at a crossroads take the B4009 straight on towards Lewknor and Watlington to a mini-roundabout by the 'Crown' then turn left into Church Road. Just past the church on the right is a small car park in front of the shopping parade. If full, find a suitable on-street parking space in nearby roads.

Chinnor at the foot of the Chiltern escarpment is now a large dormitory village swamped by modern housing estates. The rapidity of its growth can, indeed, be seen by the parish's population figures which more than quadrupled in 30 years from 1,467 in 1951 to 5,983 in 1981. Its modern appearance, however, belies the age of the village as excavations have shown that an Iron Age settlement existed on the site in the fourth century BC and traces of a Roman villa have also been found. Its church, though of Norman origin, largely dates from the fourteenth century with a slightly older tower and is notable for preserving much of its fourteenth-century work including its stained glass. It also has thirteen brasses, one of which is the oldest surviving priest brass in Britain dating from 1325, and a collection of eighteenth-century paintings by Sir James Thornhill who painted the dome of St. Paul's Cathedral. In the Civil War the village at the crossroads of the ancient Upper and Lower Icknield Ways and the mediaeval 'via regia' (royal road) from Thame to High Wycombe was sacked

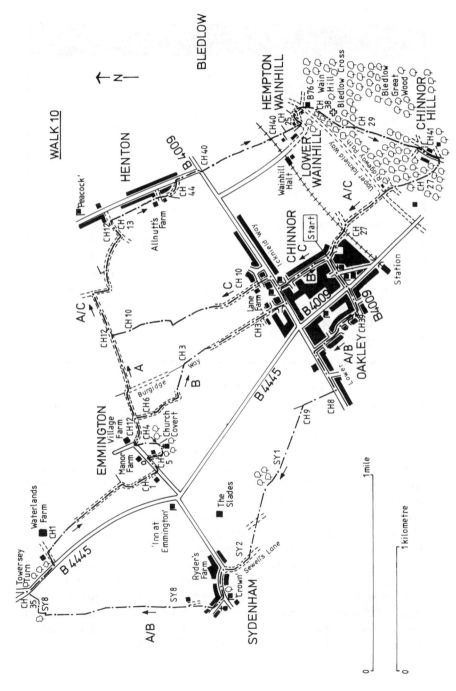

WALK 10

64

and burnt by Prince Rupert's Royalist forces in June 1643 and it later suffered a major fire in 1685 when hundreds of people were made homeless.

All three walks offer the walker something of interest. Walks A and B explore the lowlands to the northwest of Chinnor with frequent views of the Chiltern escarpment visiting the villages of Sydenham with its thatched cottages and attractive little church and Emmington, a tiny place with a couple of farms and a picturesque church which is sadly derelict, while Walks A and C circle through Henton and Hempton Wainhill before climbing the Chiltern escarpment to Chinnor Hill with its superb views across the Oxfordshire Plain and Vale of Aylesbury.

Walks A and B start at the road junction by the shopping parade and take Church Road past the shops and church to the mini-roundabout by the 'Crown'. Here take Oakley Road (B4009) straight on. After 220 yards just past house no.16 turn right onto path CH39, an alleyway leading to Cherry Tree Road then take this road straight on for a quarter-mile to a T-junction. Here turn left into Mill Lane, part of the Lower Icknield Way. Where the major road turns left, leave it and take Mill Lane straight on. 25 yards after it narrows and becomes rough, turn right over a concealed stile onto path CH8. Now follow a left-hand hedge through two fields. In the second field after 100 yards turn left over a stile, a footbridge and another stile onto path CH9, then bear half right across a field to a rail-stile left of a tin shed then bear half right with fine views of the Chiltern escarpment to your left, heading for a pylon to cross another rail-stile and footbridge. Now take path SY1 straight on beside a right-hand fence then the hedge of a copse to a rail-stile. Bear half left across the next field, with views opening out towards Sydenham ahead, Brill Hill and Long Crendon beyond and Emmington on a hillock to your right, to reach the corner of a hedge. Here ignore a crossing track and go straight on to a hedge gap into a green lane called Sewell's Lane (bridleway SY2). Turn right into this lane and follow it into Sydenham.

At a T-junction opposite some weatherboarded barns and Ryder's Farm turn left into the main village street and follow it past a picturesque row of thatched cottages. Shortly before the 'Crown' and thirteenth-century church, restored and given its wooden tower and shingle spire by John Billing in 1856, turn right into a side road. Just past a right-hand farm and a house called 'The Hedgerow' turn right onto enclosed path SY8.

On entering a paddock, turn right to cross a stile by an electricity pole then follow a right-hand fence straight on towards a thatched cottage to a gate into its garden. Keep straight on across the garden to a rail-stile then across a field to a gate and stile. Now follow a right-hand hedge straight on for two-thirds of a mile through two fields. At the far end of the second field turn right over a stile and footbridge then left and follow a left-hand hedge around two sides of a field. At the second field corner turn left over a footbridge and take path CH35 straight on across a field to a rail-stile onto the B4445 at Towersey Turn.

Turn right onto this road and after some 350 yards turn left onto path CH1, the drive to Waterlands Farm. Opposite a bungalow turn right over a culvert and follow a left-hand hedge through three fields with fine views of the Chiltern escarpment ahead. At the far end of the third field turn right then immediately left through a hedge gap and follow a left-hand hedge, now also with views behind towards Thame and Long Crendon, eventually entering a short green lane leading to the village street of Emmington. Despite only having a population of at most 80, Emmington was until 1932 a separate parish when its 44 residents and 740 acres became part of Chinnor, but its fourteenth-century church with a saddleback tower remained in use until the early 1980s. In the seventeenth century the manor was held by Richard Hampden, cousin of the Parliamentarian leader John Hampden, but his manor house is believed to have been blown up by Royalist forces when Chinnor was sacked. One unusual feature of this cul-de-sac village is that until the early nineteenth century the present road into Emmington did not exist and access to it was gained from an ancient road from Towersey to Chinnor called Burgidge Way (now path CH3) which was later closed by the Chinnor and Towersey inclosure awards.

Turn left onto the village street. After 130 yards, just past an enormous chestnut tree and opposite a concealed pond at Manor Farm, turn right onto path CH5, the drive to The Old Rectory. By this much-enlarged house bear slightly right into a green lane leading to the gates of the churchyard. Here go straight on to the door of the redundant church then take path CH4 bearing half left between a yew tree and a tall redwood to a kissing-gate and rail-stile. Now bear half left across a field towards the left-hand end of Village Farm, with a clear view of Whiteleaf Cross to your right, to cross a rail-stile by a green gate. Here turn sharp right through a second gate onto bridleway CH12, a fenced lane. Where a right-hand hedge begins, **Walk A** takes the lane straight on through a gate then, on reaching a green gate ahead, turn right then fork immediately left onto a fenced track beside a left-hand hedge. At the far end of the right-hand field take the track straight on joining Walk C. Now omit the next two paragraphs.

Where the right-hand hedge begins, **Walk B** turns right over a stile by a gate onto path CH6 following a fenced track straight on for a quarter-mile with close-up views of the Chiltern escarpment ahead, eventually turning left to reach a gate in the right-hand hedge. Turn right through this and bear half left across a field to a gate and stile in the far hedge. Cross this stile, then turn right onto path CH3. At a corner of the field go straight on over a stile and footbridge then take a grassy track beside a sporadic left-hand hedge to enter a lane on the edge of Chinnor which becomes a road and leads you to the B4009. Turn left onto this passing the 'Royal Oak' then by the 'Red Lion' turn right into High Street and follow it back to your starting point.

Walk C starts at the road junction by the shopping parade and takes High Street northwestwards for a third of a mile to a T-junction by the 'Red Lion'. Here turn right onto the B4009 towards Aylesbury. After 120 yards turn left into Holland Close. Where the macadam road ends, take path CH10 straight on along a rough lane crossing Elderdene and continuing to a gate and rail-stile into a field. Take a grassy track straight on beside a right-hand fence with fine views ahead towards the Ashendon Hills, to your right towards Whiteleaf Cross and behind you towards Wain Hill and Chinnor Hill. By a barn go straight on across a field to a corner of a hedge. Follow this hedge straight on through two fields, wiggling right at one point in the first field, to reach a gate and stile onto a fenced track (bridleway CH12). Turn right onto this joining Walk A.

Walks A and C now take this track straight on with fine views of Whiteleaf Cross, Coombe HIll and Boddington Hill ahead and Wain Hill and Chinnor Hill to your right. At a T-junction of lanes turn right and take the winding lane towards Henton for half a mile. At the edge of Henton, locally nicknamed 'Millionaires' Row' due to some expensive modern houses built in the village, just before the lane's surface becomes macadamed, turn right over a footbridge and stile onto path CH13 following a left-hand hedge straight on through an old orchard. At the far end of the orchard cross a stile and follow a left-hand fence to cross a stile in it then go straight on into a concrete farmyard at Allnutt's Farm. At the far side of the concrete turn right then immediately left beside wooden sheds to cross a stile into a paddock. Go straight on across the paddock and two gardens to the corner of a wall. Here wiggle right over a stile and go straight on crossing two more stiles to reach an unmarked fork. Now take path CH44 straight on across a lawn, passing a pergola to reach a gate into the vestiges of an old green lane known as Back Lane, then crossing another lawn and continuing along the lane which bears left to reach a road at the end of Henton.

Turn right onto this road then at a T-junction turn right onto the B4009. After 25 yards turn left over a concealed stile onto path CH40 with a fine close-up view of Wain Hill and Chinnor Hill opening out ahead. Now follow a left-hand hedge straight on towards Wain Hill for some 700 yards to the old Watlington Branch Line. Closed to passengers in 1957, the section between Princes Risborough and Chinnor was used for many years for goods traffic and is now being restored by the Chinnor and Princes Risborough Railway Association. Cross its flanking stiles and follow a right-hand fence straight on to a stile. Now follow a left-hand fence straight on uphill through four paddocks then take path CH24 straight on over a stile, through a gate and across a cottage garden to reach a rough lane (bridleway CH25). Turn left into this lane and where it forks, take the lower track straight on. Just before a gate ahead bear half right into a sunken bridleway climbing more steeply through scrubland to reach the Upper Icknield Way and Ridgeway Path opposite a large house and former pub called the 'Leather Bottle' which straddles the Buckinghamshire county boundary in the scattered hamlet of Hempton Wainhill.

Here turn right then fork immediately left onto sunken bridleway B76/CH38 which enters woodland and then (as CH38) climbs diagonally across the face of Wain Hill, later with fine views through gaps in the trees to your right. At the top of the hill ignore a branching path to your right and take bridleway CH29 straight on through scrub and across the open top of Chinnor Hill. Where views open out to your right, there is a bench about 20 yards to your right where superb views can be obtained on a clear day across Chinnor towards Didcot Power Station and the Downs to your left, the Oxford Hills and Cotswolds ahead and the Ashendon Hills to your right.

Now continue along the bridleway into and through further woodland. At a T-junction in a clearing turn left into a car park then turn right across it and take a road (CH41) straight on past some cottages. Just before a right-hand bend turn right through a squeeze-stile onto path CH27 and follow its waymarked course through the wood, soon descending a flight of steps and continuing downhill. Near the bottom, on leaving the wood, ignore a crossing path and take a green lane straight on downhill crossing the Ridgeway Path and Upper Icknield Way and continuing with fine views towards the Ashendon Hills ahead and Aylesbury to your right marked by the tall County Council office block nicknamed 'Pooley's Castle' after the former Bucks. County Council official who built it. After a quarter-mile at a fork bear left, soon crossing a railway level-crossing and continuing down Keens Lane to your starting point.

WALK 11: CUXHAM

Length of Walk: 6.8 miles / 10.9 Km
Starting Point: Village end of B480 layby east of Cuxham.
Grid Ref: SU670953
Maps: OS Landranger Sheets 164 or Sheets 165 & 175
OS Explorer Sheet 171 (or old Sheet 3)
OS Pathfinder Sheet 1137 (SU69/79)

How to get there / Parking: Cuxham, 7 miles south of Thame, may be reached from the town by taking the A329 towards Wallingford to Stadhampton. Here turn left onto the B480 towards Watlington. On reaching Cuxham, take the B480 straight on through the village. Just beyond the end of the village turn left into an unmarked layby keeping right at a fork and parking where it is wide enough for other vehicles to pass.

Cuxham, pronounced 'Cooksem', in a hollow on the Oxford–Watlington road, is a small unspoilt village with a babbling brook alongside its village street of picturesque thatched cottages. The village, much of which for centuries belonged to Merton Collage, Oxford, also has a Norman church which was heavily restored in about 1700 with its original font and Jacobean pulpit.

The walk explores the gently rolling hills around Cuxham with superb views in places of the Chiltern escarpment. It also visits Brightwell Baldwin with its beautiful sylvan park, Chalgrove with it fine church, thatched cottages and roadside brook sadly swamped by modern development, Chalgrove Field with its monument to John Hampden, the most prominent casualty of its Civil War battle and the tiny deserted hillside village of Easington.

Starting from the Cuxham end of the B480 layby east of the village, take the B480 into Cuxham. Just past the 'Half Moon' turn left over a bridge then right onto a path between a stone wall and the brook. By a telephone box and the next bridge bear slightly left into a walled alleyway leading you to a road by the church. Turn left onto this road passing the church and entering a farmyard at Manor Farm. Here take path CX5 straight on along a fenced track winding its way uphill. Where the enclosing hedges end, turn right leaving the track and following a right-hand hedge with views across the village to your right then gradually bearing left, now with views of Brightwell Baldwin and Didcot Power Station to your right and the Chiltern escarpment over your left shoulder. On reaching a hedge gap into Turners Green Lane (bridleway BR3/CX1, later BB7/CX1), turn right into it gently descending for a third of a mile to reach a road opposite a lodge of Brightwell Park. Turn left onto this road and follow it for a quarter-mile passing a fine row of lime trees and entering Brightwell Baldwin village.

Brightwell Baldwin is a village with its church, fifteenth-century inn and cottages scattered along one long street bordering the Park. Its thirteenth-century church is particularly notable for a wealth of fifteenth-century stained glass. It also has some seventeenth-century glass depicting the arms of John Howson and the Sees of Oxford and Durham, both of whose bishoprics he at one time held. The church also contains an eight-foot-long brass from 1439 marking Sir John Cottesmore, a fifteenth-century Chief Justice and a baroque memorial to the Stone family of Brightwell Park. Their house, which was rebuilt in about 1790, in common with mansions at Ascott (near Stadhampton) and Wheatfield, was destroyed by fire and subsequently the stable block was made into the house we see today. In 1991 an attempt was made to secure planning permission to convert part of Brightwell Park into a golf course, but following local protests South Oxfordshire District Council rejected the application which would have ruined the Park's secluded charm.

Opposite the thatched Glebe Farm turn right over a stile by a gate into Brightwell Park and take path BB4 bearing slightly left, passing just left of a group of three chestnut trees and continuing to a kissing-gate right of an enormous storm-damaged cedar where there is a good view of the house to your left. Now keep straight on, passing a seventeenth-century dovecote some distance to your right, to reach a kissing-gate by a white gate then continue through a further gate into a belt of woodland. At the far side of the wood cross a stile by a gate and bear slightly left across a large arable field, soon heading just right of Cadwell Farm ahead to reach the left-hand end of a hedge. Here keep straight on across the next field to a gap between a poplar and a willow then turn left onto a mown grassy track. At a track junction turn left over a culvert then right into Cadwell Lane, a macadam farm road (bridleway BB1, later CG13). Take this straight on for nearly half a mile passing through a copse, beyond which Chalgrove's Norman church with a fourteenth-century tower noted for its fourteenth-century wall paintings comes into view ahead. Just before a left-hand bend turn right over a stile onto path CG14 bearing half left and following a right-hand hedge to reach a stile onto Berrick Road at Chalgrove.

Turn right onto this road. Where it forks, turn right over a bridge then right again onto path CG15, a grassy track between hedges into a field. Now follow a right-hand yew, later beech hedge straight on. Where the hedge bears right, leave it bearing half left across a field to a hedge gap into a plantation. Take an obvious path straight on through the plantation, soon entering another field with a view of the Chiltern escarpment opening out ahead. Here keep straight on towards Shirburn Hill, an outcrop of the escarpment, to reach a stile onto the B480. Cross this, bearing slightly right and take a largely disused road (the former route of the B480 before the wartime airfield and modern Chalgrove Bypass led to its abandonment), bearing left and following it for two-thirds of a mile to a crossroads by the Hampden Monument.

This monument was erected in 1843 to mark the bicentenary of the Civil War Battle of Chalgrove Field, at which John Hampden, one of the leaders of the Parliamentary side, was mortally wounded not far from this spot. On the other side of the crossroads this military theme is continued by a second smaller monument to American airmen stationed at the nearby Chalgrove Airfield in World War II.

Here turn right into Warpsgrove Lane which ultimately leads to the lost village of Warpsgrove. This hamlet was once large enough to have its own church but now comprises a mere two or three scattered cottages. After a third of a mile where the road's right-hand footway ends, turn right onto bridleway CG16, a macadam road at first, which soon turns left. Where it forks, take a macadam road straight on. At its end by some factory gates go straight on into a field and follow a grassy track. After about 250 yards, where the track ends at double gates into a plantation, turn right across the field to a metal gate at the corner of a hedge. Go through this and take an old green lane straight on. (N.B. If the green lane is impassable, keep right of the gate and walk parallel to the green lane to rejoin the official route at the next field corner.) On entering a field where Easington comes into view ahead, keep straight on to a gap in the next hedge. (From here to Easington it is currently

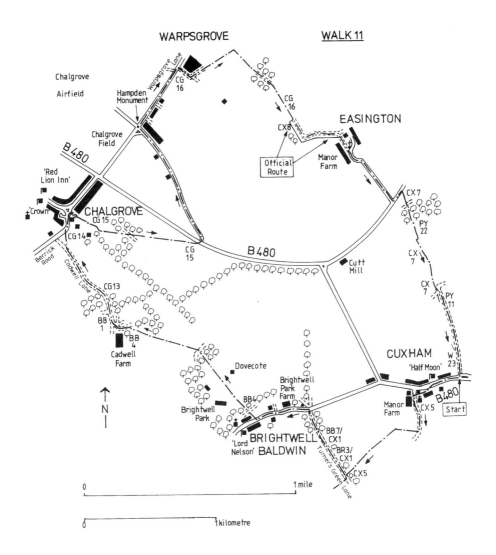

necessary to take an unofficial diversion, the official route being shown on the plan. Please observe any waymarking encountered.) Now take the unofficial route of bridleway CX8 straight on through a gate and along a track uphill, later bearing left to reach a track junction near Manor Farm. Here (rejoining the official route) turn right onto a track uphill between farm buildings, soon with a concrete surface, to reach a bend in the public road at Easington.

Easington, once a separate parish, has a small thirteenth-century church with a bell-turret, Norman font and Jacobean pulpit round a bend to your left. Aerial photographs reveal that this cul-de-sac village which now comprises little more than a large farm and a church, like others in this area, was once much larger but possibly the plague or early enclosure led to its depopulation.

Take this road straight on over a hill with wide views of the Chiltern escarpment from Beacon Hill to Ewelme Down opening out ahead. At a T-junction turn left then after 100 yards turn right through a gap in the hedge and roadside bank onto path CX7 following a left-hand hedge downhill. At a corner of the field take path PY22 straight on through a hedge gap and across a track into a belt of scrub. Keep straight on through this then follow a right-hand hedge to cross a footbridge. Now continue beside the right-hand hedge through a second field into a third. In the third field after 60 yards transfer through a gap in the hedge and take path CX7 along its other side to the far end of the hedge. Here bear slightly left to join a macadam farm road (bridleway PY11) and follow it straight on over a hill with views over your right shoulder towards the Oxford Hills then descending steeply (now on bridleway W23) to reach the layby on the edge of Cuxham.

Length of Walk: (Basic) 8.1 miles / 13.1 Km
(Detour to Littletown) + 0.7 miles / 1.1 Km
(Via Long Wittenham Church) + 0.1 miles / 0.2 Km

Starting Point: Entrance to Wittenham Clumps car park.

Grid Ref: SU567924

Maps: OS Landranger Sheet 174
OS Explorer Sheet 170
OS Pathfinder Sheet 1136 (SU49/59)

How to get there / Parking: Wittenham Clumps, 3 miles north-west of Wallingford, may be reached from the town by taking the A4130 towards Didcot. Having passed Brightwell-cum-Sotwell, turn right onto the Wittenhams and Appleford road then after half a mile turn right onto the Wittenham Clumps and Little Wittenham road and follow it to a signposted car park on the right.

Notes: This walk should not be attempted when the Thames is in flood.

Wittenham Clumps is the popular name given to two of the Sinodun Hills capped by clumps of beech trees. Though privately owned, the area around the Clumps is open to the public subject to the presentation of a single red rose to the owner on the site each summer. Historically of strategic importance due to the panoramic views these hills afford of the surrounding Thames valley, the Clumps, one of which is also capped by a substantial Bronze Age hill fort, overlook Dorchester-on-Thames which excavations have proved to have been inhabited for some 5,000 years. Following the Roman invasion in 43 AD a Roman road was built from Silchester in Hampshire to Alchester near Bicester crossing the Thames near Dorchester and a fortified town known as Dorocina was built to defend it on the site of the modern village in about 70 AD. After the Romans left in the fifth century, Dorchester soon became a Saxon town and seems by the seventh century to have become capital of the Saxon Kingdom of Wessex. In 634 it was here that the Christian missionary, Bishop Birinus converted King Cynegils to

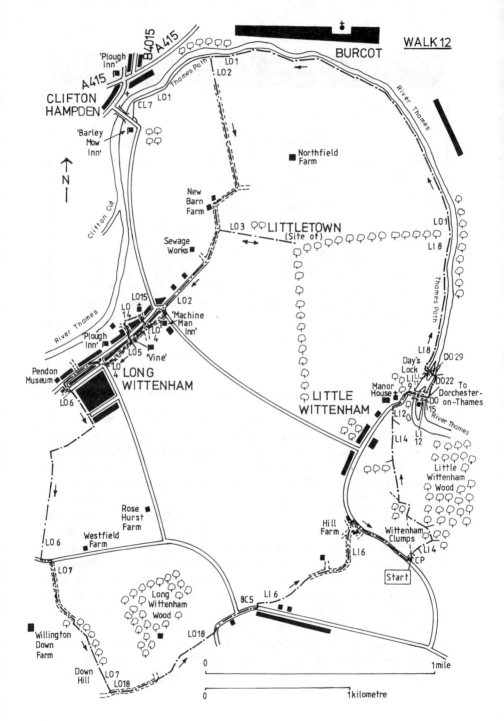

BURCOT

CLIFTON HAMPDEN

'Plough Inn'

A415

B4015

A415

'Barley Mow Inn'

Thames Path

LO 1

LO 2

CL 7

LO 1

N

Clifton Cut

River Thames

Northfield Farm

New Barn Farm

Sewage Works

LO 3

LITTLETOWN
(Site of)

River Thames

Thames Path

LO 1

LI 8

LO15

LO 14

LO 2

'Machine Man Inn'

LO 4

LO 5

'Vine'

LO 4

'Plough Inn'

Pendon Museum

LONG WITTENHAM

LO 6

LITTLE WITTENHAM

Manor House

Day's Lock

LI 18

LI 11

LI 9

DO 15

DO 22

DO 29

To Dorchester-on-Thames

River Thames

LI 12

LI 14

LI 12

Little Wittenham Wood

Rose Hurst Farm

Westfield Farm

LO 6

LO 7

Long Wittenham Wood

Willington Down Farm

LO 7

LO 18

Down Hill

Hill Farm

LI 16

Wittenham Clumps

LI 14

CP

Start

BC 5

LI 6

LO 18

0   1 mile

0   1 kilometre

76

Christianity and made Dorchester his episcopal see, building a cathedral where Dorchester Abbey now stands. In 705, however, the Wessex capital moved to Winchester and the importance of Dorchester gradually declined. Following the Norman conquest the bishopric was moved to Lincoln and in about 1140 the now ruinous cathedral was replaced by Dorchester Abbey which today dominates the village when looking from the Clumps. In 1536 its church was spared destruction following the Reformation as Abbot Beauforest bought it for the village for £140. Due to the considerable cost of its upkeep, this huge church, famous for its twelfth-century glass, its Jesse window and its rare lead font, has survived largely unaltered to this day.

The walk explores this landscape rich in beauty and historical interest crossing the top of the Clumps before dropping to Little Wittenham and the Thames. You now follow the Thames towpath over Day's Lock and past Burcot almost to the picturesque village of Clifton Hampden (well worth a detour) then turn inland with an optional detour to the site of the lost hamlet of Littletown destroyed in 1838, before reaching the beautiful riverside village of Long Wittenham. The walk then leads you up Down Hill and returns with almost constant wide views to Wittenham Clumps car park.

Starting from the entrance to Wittenham Clumps car park with its fine views towards the Downs and Chilterns, turn right through gates into the Little Wittenham Nature Reserve and take path LI4 following a right-hand fence. Where the fence turns right, leave it and continue uphill, soon climbing the ramparts of the Bronze Age hill fort. Disregard branching paths to left and right and continue into a copse forming the lower of the Clumps. In the copse turn left onto a branching path (still LI4) soon emerging with a fine view to your right across the Thames valley towards Dorchester Abbey. Here continue across a field and descend a flight of steps in the ramparts of the hill fort then climb again ignoring a branching path to your right and crossing a stile. Now follow a right-hand fence straight on, disregarding a stile and gates to your right, and continue uphill with fine views towards the Downs to your left and across Dorchester towards the Oxford Hills to your right to reach a fence surrounding the higher of the two clumps. Here turn right and follow this fence now additionally with views to your right towards the

Chilterns, gradually bearing left to reach a seat and direction-finder provided by the AA in 1980. Having admired the panoramic views, turn right (still on path LI4) and descend steeply towards Little Wittenham Church passing through a kissing-gate and following a left-hand hedge, later joining bridleway LI2 to reach gates and a V-stile opposite the manor house and church which was largely rebuilt in 1863 but retains its fourteenth-century tower.

Here turn right into the village street which soon becomes byway LI9 and descends to cross first a backwater then the weir stream of the Thames to reach an island. Now take bridleway LI12 (soon becoming DO15) straight on across a bridge over the main stream with views towards Dorchester Abbey ahead to a gate on the far bank. Here turn left onto the Thames Path (DO22) and follow it to Day's Lock, near where there has been a weir and some sort of lock since 1580. Ignore a gate at the near end of the lock then at its far end turn left through a kissing-gate and take path DO29 across the lock. Now take path LI11 over a causeway over the weir back to the former Berkshire bank. Here go through a gate, turn right onto the towpath (now LI8, later LO1) and follow it for two miles soon with views of Wittenham Clumps behind you and later passing Burcot, one-time home of the late Poet Laureate, John Masefield on the far bank. Having passed a black-and-white boathouse with a tall flagpole at Burcot on the opposite bank, continue to the next fenceline.

Here, if wishing to visit Clifton Hampden with its historic thatched 'Barley Mow Inn' made famous in 1889 by its depiction in Jerome K Jerome's 'Three Men in a Boat', its brick bridge built in 1864 by the celebrated architect George Gilbert Scott to replace a ferry, its twelfth-century church restored by the same architect and its picturesque thatched cottages, take the Thames Path (LO1, later CL7) for a further half-mile looking out for a garden on the other bank with pillars bearing some of the weather-beaten heads from outside the Sheldonian in Oxford replaced by new ones in the 1970s.

Otherwise, leaving the Thames Path, **DO NOT** cross the stile but turn left onto path LO2 following a right-hand fence over a long floodwalk to a gate and stile into a green lane. Take this lane straight on for half a mile to a macadam farm road. Turn right onto this rounding a left-hand bend by New Barn Farm. At a slight right-hand bend cul-de-sac path LO3 to your left leads you through a hedge gap and across a field to the site of the lost hamlet of Littletown at the near end of a line of tall poplars, although there is now little trace of it except for bricks and the outlines of houses visible when the field is not in crop. Now continue along the farm road for almost half a mile to a T-junction with a public road on the edge of Long Wittenham, which has been inhabited since the Iron Age and where a Saxon cemetery has been found with a large number of soldiers buried with their weapons.

Here turn left then at a slight left-hand bend turn right onto a gravel road (LO4) passing the 'Machine Man Inn' and continuing past the backs of gardens. At a staggered junction with a crossing farm track, if wishing to see the church (built in about 1120 of stone imported from Caen in Normandy on the site of an ancient barrow, with a fifteenth-century tower and a rare lead font hidden in the Civil War to prevent its being melted down to make bullets), turn right onto gravel road LO16 to reach the High Street. Now take gravel road LO15 straight on past a thatched timber-framed cottage with jutting upper storey and a fine thatched weatherboarded barn to the churchyard gates. Here turn left through a kissing-gate onto path LO14 along the edge of the churchyard then continuing to a kissing-gate. Now bear left to join a macadam drive onto which you turn left to reach the High Street opposite the 'Vine'. Bear slightly right across the road and take path LO5 at the side of the pub past a timber-framed wall to a crossing grassy track (LO4 again), onto which you turn right.

Otherwise, at the staggered junction fork left then right along a track past back gardens (still LO4) with views of Wittenham Clumps in places to your left **soon rejoining the alternative route** and continuing to Didcot Road. Turn right onto this then by a Saxon cross fork immediately left and at a T-junction turn left again into the attractive High Street which leads to the Pendon Museum with its model 1930s landscapes and railway memorabilia. By the post office turn left then where the road turns left again, take path LO6 straight on beside a left-hand fence. Ignore a branching path into a housing estate and continue to the far side of the field then turn right and follow a left-hand fence, later a hedge looking out for a concealed footbridge to your left. Turn left over this and follow a sporadic left-hand hedge for half a mile, with views to your left towards Wittenham Clumps in places, to reach a road. Turn left onto this then after some 70 yards turn right onto bridleway LO7 along a grassy track beside a right-hand hedge, later a fence through two fields. At the far side of the second field go straight on over a stile by a bridlegate then bear half right to enter the right-hand field. Here turn left and follow its left-hand hedge to the top of Down Hill where a fine view opens out through a hedge gap ahead towards the Downs and Chilterns.

Do **NOT** go through this hedge gap but turn left onto path LO18 taking a grassy track beside a right-hand hedge. Where the track turns left, leave it and follow the right-hand hedge straight on for a third of a mile, later with views to your left towards the white buildings of Culham Laboratory, to reach a bend in the Moretons road. Take this road straight on to a T-junction where you fork right onto the Wallingford road. After about 170 yards just past a cottage called 'Haddon Close Orchard', turn left through a hedge gap onto path BC5 crossing a narrow enclosure to a stile where wide views open out towards the Oxford Hills to your left and Wittenham Clumps to your right. Cross this stile and turn right onto path LI6 following a right-hand hedge to cross another stile then follow a right-hand fence straight on with additional views to your right towards Brightwell Barrow with its small clump of trees, the Chilterns and later the Downs. Having crossed a further stile, take a grassy track straight on beside a left-hand fence at first then continuing across a field gradually bearing left to reach Hill Farm. Here take a concrete track straight on ignoring two branching tracks to your left then dropping to a road. Turn sharp right onto this road and follow it uphill with fine views to your right towards the Downs to reach your starting point.

WALK 13:   WALLINGFORD

Length of Walk: 6.2 miles / 10.0 Km
Starting Point: Wallingford Town Hall.
Grid Ref: SU607894
Maps: OS Landranger Sheets 174 & 175
OS Explorer Sheet 170
OS Pathfinder Sheets 1136 (SU49/59),
1137 (SU69/79), 1155 (SU48/58) &
1156 (SU68/78)
Parking: There are several car parks in the town and at the
eastern end of Wallingford Bridge.
Notes: This walk should not be attempted when the Thames is
in flood, as parts of it are prone to flooding.

Wallingford, on the banks of the Thames just above where it enters
the Chilterns, was for centuries a strategic river crossing. Its ford,
first mentioned in a chronical of 821, was guarded in Saxon times by
a walled town which in 1066 was where William the Conqueror
crossed the Thames on his circuitous progression towards London.
In 1071 Robert D'Oilly built a castle here, which in 1142 gave refuge
to Queen Matilda on her flight from Oxford to Normandy, the
foundations and some ramparts of which can still be seen today.
The importance of Wallingford can be seen by the fact that it was
granted a charter as early as 1155 when there were no fewer than ten
churches within the town walls. Today only three remain: St. Mary's
behind the Town Hall rebuilt in 1854 but retaining its fifteenth-
century tower, St. Peter's completely rebuilt in 1777 with a unique
hollow spire and St. Leonard's rebuilt after serious damage in the
Civil War but retaining some Saxon herringbone stone-work and
Norman arches. Another casualty of the Civil War was Wallingford
Castle which, having withstood a 65-day siege by Parliamentary
forces, was demolished on Cromwell's orders. Today the town,
which has a picturesque centre preserving its Saxon street pattern,
is characterised by the elegant spire of St. Peter's and the graceful
seventeen-arched bridge rebuilt in 1809 on thirteenth-century
foundations and finally bypassed by the A4130 in 1993.

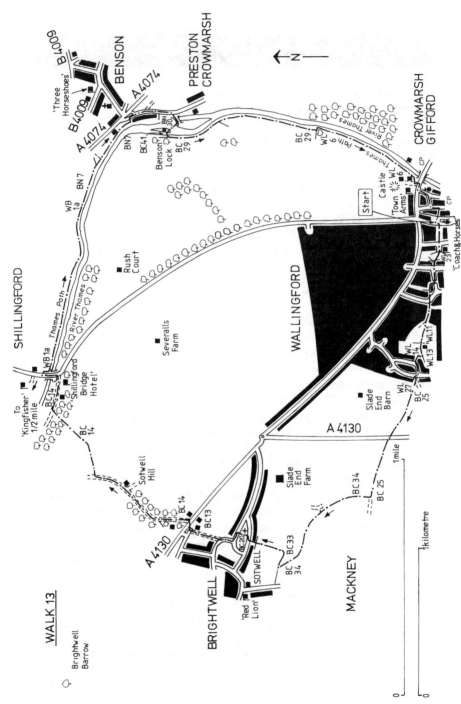

WALK 13

Brightwell
Barrow

The walk takes you across Kinecroft Park and the Saxon fortifications before leaving the town and crossing some flat fields with fine views of the Downs and Chilterns to reach the picturesque village of Sotwell. You then climb to the top of Sotwell Hill where superb views open out towards the Chilterns and Ashendon Hills before dropping to cross the Thames by Shillingford's graceful bridge and take the towpath back by way of Benson to Wallingford.

Starting at the front of Wallingford's fine town hall of 1670, go past its right side. By the Church of St. Mary-le-More turn right along Church Lane to Goldsmith's Lane then take a road called Kinecroft straight on to the 'Coach and Horses'. Now take macadam path WL23 bearing slightly right across Kinecroft Park to a gap in the Saxon town fortifications leading to a footbridge and Croft Road. Cross this and take path WL11 straight on along a road called Croft Villas. At its end just before a vehicle barrier, turn right onto a macadam path round the back of some garages bearing left and ignoring branching paths to right and left. Now cross Charter Way and take a macadam path straight on, soon becoming fenced. Disregard a crossing path and continue along path WL13. Where wooden garden fences begin to your right, turn right onto macadam path WL14 soon bearing left into Greenfield Crescent. Turn left onto this road then at a T-junction turn right into Firtree Avenue then immediately left onto path WL27, a wide macadam alleyway to some allotments. By the entrance to the allotments fork right through a kissing-gate and take enclosed path BC25 for 250 yards to a footbridge into a field. Here bear slightly right and follow a right-hand hedge then continue to a stile onto the A4130 Wallingford Bypass.

Bear slightly right across this road to a stile and footbridge virtually opposite with views opening out towards the Downs to your left, Brightwell Barrow and Wittenham Clumps to your right and across the town towards the Chiltern escarpment behind you. Now bear slightly right across a field towards an electricity pole and Didcot Power Station to reach a fence gap and culvert. Cross the culvert then turn right over a stile onto path BC34 following a right-hand stream for over a third of a mile, with fine views of Wittenham Clumps and Brightwell Barrow ahead and across Wallingford to the Chilterns to your right, ignoring two culverts over the stream and gradually bearing left. At the far end of the field cross a culvert and continue beside the right-hand stream. Where the stream turns right, leave it and bear half right across the field to a kissing-gate in the far corner. Do NOT go through it but turn sharp right onto path BC33 beside a left-hand stream to cross a culvert at the next field corner and follow a left-hand fence. Where the fence turns sharp left, leave it and bear slightly left across the field to cross a stile by the left-hand end of a brick-and-flint wall. Here ignore a crossing path and take an enclosed path straight on to Sotwell village street.

Turn right onto it passing 'Dobsons', a seventeenth-century brick-and-timber cottage then turn left through the churchyard gates onto path BC20. Now follow the left-hand edge of the churchyard past the church to a gate into Akers Lane. Turn left onto this road and at a fork, keep right. Where the road bears sharp left, leave it and take bridleway BC13 straight on up a macadam drive into a green lane, eventually joining another drive and reaching a cul-de-sac road. Turn right between bollards then bear half left across a verge to cross the A4130 and enter bridleway BC14, a green lane right of a macadam drive. Take this sunken way gently uphill for a third of a mile to enter fields at the top of Sotwell Hill with superb views across the Thames Valley towards Brill Hill ahead and an extensive length of the Chiltern escarpment to your right. Here join a farm track and continue along it, soon bearing left. 120 yards beyond the left-hand bend, turn right across a field to reach the tall pylon of a crossing powerline then bear half left across the next field to the left side of a copse. Here take a defined path near a left-hand fence steeply downhill through a plantation with a view across the Thames towards Shillingford ahead. At the bottom of the hill turn right onto a farm road and follow it through the car park of the Shillingford Bridge Hotel to the old main road.

Turn left onto this road crossing Shillingford Bridge built in 1827 on the site of an earlier bridge to carry the Aylesbury–Wallingford turnpike road. Just past the far end of its parapet turn sharp right onto fenced path WB1a (the Thames Path) following the side of the bridge back to the riverbank. Now turn left and take a fenced path along the riverbank, eventually emerging into meadows with views of the Chilterns ahead. At the far end of the second meadow go through a small gate and cross a footbridge, then take path BN7 still following the riverbank and soon passing a caravan site. At the far end of the caravan site walk round a slipway and continue along the riverbank past a shop and cafe into a small park. At the far side of the park by the concrete remnants of the former ferry moorings turn left to a gate into Preston Crowmarsh Lane then turn right for a T-junction where Benson's thirteenth-century church with an eighteenth-century tower can be seen to your left.

Benson, in mediaeval times a royal manor known as Bensington, was the site of a ford used by the Romans and in AD 777 was the scene of a battle in which King Offa of Mercia defeated the forces of Wessex. In 1736 the routing of the Henley–Oxford turnpike road through the village led to its prosperity and a proliferation of coaching inns, but the construction of a bypass in about 1930 and RAF Benson just before the war in 1939 with the resultant closure of road accesses from the south made Benson into a quiet backwater and so most of the inns have since closed.

At the T-junction turn right into the Preston Crowmarsh road. After some 300 yards by a Thames Path signpost turn right through a small gate onto fenced macadam path BN30, soon crossing footbridges over a Thames backwater and Benson Weir then continue across a narrow island to Benson Lock. Here take path BC41 across the lock gates then turn left onto path BC29 (the Thames towpath) and follow it down-stream for two-thirds of a mile. On reaching a group of three gates, go straight on through a bridlegate and take fenced towpath WL6 for a further half mile with the spire of St. Peter's Church coming into view ahead and later passing the ruins of Wallingford Castle to your right. On nearing Wallingford Bridge, follow the path bearing right between walls to reach Castle Lane then turn left and cross High Street by the 'Town Arms'. Turn right onto its pavement then immediately left into Thames Street. Now, leaving the Thames Path, turn right into St. Peter's Street then left into Wood Lane. After 65 yards just before a red-brick terrace to your right, turn right into a narrow alley called Mousey Lane which leads to your starting point.

Length of Walk: (A)   8.5 miles / 13.8 Km
                      (B)   5.2 miles / 8.3 Km
Starting Point: Gates to Cholsey churchyard.
Grid Ref: SU584870
Maps: OS Landranger Sheet 174
                      OS Explorer Sheet 170
                      OS Pathfinder Sheet 1155 (SU48/58)

How to get there / Parking: Cholsey Church, 2 miles southwest of Wallingford, may be reached from the town by taking the road towards Reading. At the Winterbrook Roundabouts first turn right onto the A4130 towards Didcot then turn left onto the Cholsey road. In the village, having passed the 'Red Lion', at a mini-roundabout turn right into Church Road towards South Moreton and Didcot. After crossing a hump-backed railway bridge, turn left into the church approach and park on the right facing the fence.

Cholsey in the Thames Valley at the foot of the Downs is today a large modern commuter dormitory built around its railway station, but this belies the village's considerable history, as 1,000 years ago it became the site of an abbey built by King Ethelred II to atone for the death of his half-brother, King Edward the Martyr, who is said to have been murdered at the instigation of Queen Elfrida, Ethelred's mother in 978. 100 years earlier the Danish King Bacseg stayed in Cholsey after sacking Wallingford but in the battle which ensued on Blewburton Hill, he was defeated and slain by King Ethelred I and the future King Alfred of Wessex. Cholsey Abbey did not survive for long, however, as another Danish attack resulted in the destruction of both village and abbey, but during Victorian restoration work on the Norman parish church, in whose churchyard the authoress Dame Agatha Mary Clarissa Mallowan (1890–1976) is buried (better known as Agatha Christie, creator of Miss Marple and Hercule Poirot), scorch marks found on some of the ancient stones showed that stone from the Saxon abbey had been used in the building of the church.

Both walks lead you from Cholsey to circle Lollingdon Hill, a foothill of the Downs with fine views, before continuing to the picturesque village of Aston Tirrold with its thatched cottages. From here Walk A continues through the village to the top of Blewburton Hill with its Iron Age hill fort, site of the ancient battle where even better views can be obtained before returning to Cholsey via the pretty village of South Moreton and Cholsey Hill with its open views, while Walk B takes a direct route back to Cholsey.

Walks A and B start from the gates to Cholsey churchyard and take a macadam path passing left of the church then bearing left through a gap in a wall to a stile in the outer wall of the churchyard. Here take path CS17 bearing slightly right across a field to cross a stile and footbridge in the far corner by the Wallingford Branch Line. Now follow the fence of this railway, a victim of the Beeching axe now in the hands of a preservation society, through a field and a belt of scrub until you reach a fence gap leading to a concrete path at the end of a subway under the branch line.

Here turn right onto path CS4 over a culvert, soon passing through a long tunnel under the old GWR main line. At the far end of the tunnel by the parapet of a culvert turn left onto path CS5 bearing half right across a field with views of the Downs gradually opening out ahead. At the far side of the field cross a footbridge and take what is normally a crop break straight on, bearing slightly right at a former hedge line and continuing to a hedge gap near a pylon. Here cross a green lane, go through another hedge gap and follow the left side of a hedge straight on under the pylon. At the far end of the field go through a hedge gap then bear slightly right along what is normally a crop break passing right of an electricity pole to cross a footbridge and stile. Keep straight on across the next field to pass through a hedge gap right of an ash tree then follow a right-hand fence to a gate and stile onto a macadam farm road (bridleway CS6) near Lollingdon Farm.

Turn left onto the macadam road. Where it bears right, follow it (now on bridleway CS7) climbing the side of Lollingdon Hill with several changes of surface and views opening out behind you towards the Sinodun Hills and Didcot Power Station, then descending again with views of the Downs ahead. Where the right-hand fence briefly gives way to a hedge, turn right and take fenced path CS23 beside a left-hand hedge. At the far end of the hedge follow a right-hand fence straight on along the foot of Lollingdon Hill with fine views of the Downs to your left. At the far end of the left-hand field pass some gates and join path CS11, a grassy track, bearing slightly right uphill soon with a fence to your left and views towards Didcot and the Sinodun Hills ahead. On reaching a copse, turn sharp left onto bridleway CS12 crossing a field diagonally to a gate at the near end of a hedge. (If bridleway CS12 is still obstructed, retrace your steps to the corner of the fence then turn right and follow the fence to the gate.)

Go through the gate and take path AT14 bearing half right across the next field heading for the left-hand end of Didcot Power Station to reach a fence gap leading to fenced bridleway AT7. Turn left onto the bridleway then after some 350 yards by a rail-stile in the left-hand fence, fork right onto path AT3, a green lane which soon bears left. Where the lane ends, take a grassy track (now path AT5) straight on beside a left-hand fence then a hedge with views of Aston Tirrold with its part Saxon church with a fifteenth-century tower to your left. On passing a metal gate, **Walk A** turns left onto path AT4 taking the track which becomes a concrete road to Aston Street in Aston Tirrold. Now omit the next paragraph.

On passing the gate, **Walk B** turns right through a kissing-gate onto path AT4 bearing half left across a field to a kissing-gate and culvert in the right-hand gap in a belt of poplar trees. Now turn right through a kissing-gate by a gate onto a concrete track beside the tree belt with fine views towards Cholsey Church and the Chilterns ahead. Where the track and tree belt end, go straight on over a stile and take a fenced path beside a stream past one field. On entering a second field, turn left beside a left-hand fence then keep right of a ditch and follow it to the far side of the field. Here turn right and follow a left-hand hedge and stream to a footbridge. Turn left over this then right onto path CS4 to reach a corner of a field. Here turn left onto path CS18 taking a grassy track towards a farm with fine views ahead then join a farm road at a bend and follow it straight on for half a mile passing right of the farm and over a railway bridge then on to Manor Farm. At the farm go past a black barn then by the start of a left-hand plantation turn right across a field to a corner of the churchyard wall. Here cross a stile and pass left of the church noting the particularly large headstone of the grave of Agatha Christie and her husband then bearing right to the gates at your starting point.

Walk A turns left into Aston Street passing Races Farm then turns right onto path AT1 up steps and through gates into Aston Tirrold churchyard taking a gravel path passing left of the church and entering an alleyway. Take this alleyway straight on through the village crossing Rectory Lane and Baker Street and reaching a bend in Spring Lane by a nonconformist chapel built in 1726 on the site of the oldest such chapel in England founded in 1662. Here take Spring Lane, the boundary between Aston Tirrold and the racehorse-training village of Aston Upthorpe, straight on then at a left-hand bend fork right up some steps onto fenced path AU5. At the far end of the field you enter a green lane then take bridleway AU4 straight on beside a right-hand fence along the foot of Blewburton Hill with fine views along the Downs to your left and towards the Chilterns behind you. Ignore the first stile in the right-hand fence then at the far end of the field turn right over a second stile (where five kestrels were seen in 1993) and take a permissive path beside a right-hand fence steeply up Blewburton Hill with views of Blewbury to your left and the Chilterns to your right. Where the fence turns right, follow it later bearing left to reach a concrete triangulation post at the top of the hill where there are panoramic views in all directions. (NB If the permissive path is closed, take fenced bridleway BL10 straight on for 200 yards then turn right over a stile onto path BL3 and use path BL37 as a cul-de-sac to reach the top of the hill.)

Now turn left onto path BL37 aiming for the right-hand end of Blewbury and soon descending steeply, noticing the pronounced ramparts of the Iron Age hill fort. On reaching the bottom fence, turn right onto path BL3 following it until you cross a stile in it where it is currently necessary to take an unofficial route beside a right-hand hedge towards Wittenham Clumps to reach Hagbourne Road on the edge of Aston Upthorpe. (In order to avoid difficulties, walkers are advised to heed any waymarks on this section.)

Turn right onto this road passing a seat. After 100 yards turn left through a kissing-gate onto path BL39 following a right-hand hedge past a series of paddocks for a third of a mile. Where a central hedge divides the path into two, keep right of it and take an enclosed path straight on for another half a mile with views towards South Moreton ahead and the Chilterns to your right, passing a picnic table and continuing to a kissing-gate onto fenced bridleway BL16. Here bear half right across the bridleway to cross a stile by a gate onto path AU11 following a left-hand fence to a stile and footbridge to your left. Do NOT cross these but turn right onto path AU9 heading towards South Moreton Church to join the bank of Mill Brook and follow it to a stile. Turn left over this soon crossing a footbridge then take path SM8 along the bank of the brook through a paddock past the heavily-restored thirteenth-century church with a Saxon doorway to reach a stile and footbridge. Cross these then turn left onto path SM6 crossing a second footbridge and ignoring a path to your left. Where the right-hand wall ends, turn right onto enclosed path SM9 then where a concrete wall bars your way ahead, turn left reaching the end of a road by a farm gate and continuing along it to South Moreton village street.

Here bear half right crossing the road and taking path SM11 along a rough lane left of the 'Crown'. On leaving the village, take a green lane straight on, passing through gates, then bearing right and continuing to a tunnel under the old GWR main line. At the far end of the tunnel turn right onto a grassy track ignoring a branching track to your left and crossing a bridge into the next field. Now bear half left across it to a stile and footbridge by a dead willow tree where there are views to your left towards North Moreton Church and the Sinodun Hills. Turn right over this bridge onto path SM12 then turn left and follow the sewage works fence. By a corner of the works turn right through a fence gap then left and follow a left-hand stream and sporadic hedge for three-quarters of a mile with views towards Wallingford and the Chilterns ahead and later the Sinodun Hills to your left and ignoring a hunt bridge to your left. At the far end of the field cross a stile and footbridge then bear left onto path CS21. After 15 yards ignore a rail-stile in the left-hand fence and take path CS22 following a left-hand hedge to cross a stile by gates onto a road called Hithercroft.

Cross this road bearing slightly right and following a crop break up Cholsey Hill. At the far end of the crop break, where there are panoramic views towards the Chilterns ahead and to your left, the Downs to your right and the Sinodun Hills behind you, bear half right across a large field heading just left of a line of pylons on the skyline to reach Church Road. Turn left onto this road passing Cholsey Manor and Manor Farm with its fine brick-and-flint and weatherboarded barns to reach your starting point.

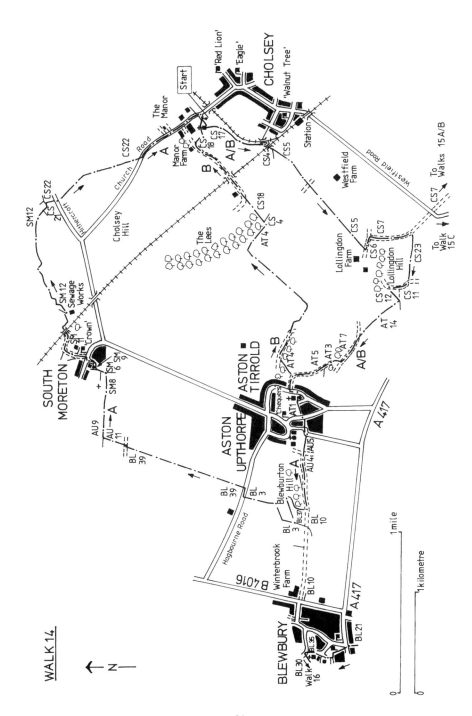

WALK 14

←N—

91

WALK 15:   MOULSFORD

Length of Walk: (A) 7.8 miles / 12.6 Km
                     (B) 2.9 miles / 4.7 Km
                     (C) 5.5 miles / 8.8 Km
Starting Point: (A/B) Telephone box by Moulsford
                            Recreation Ground.
                     (C)   A417 crossroads at Kingstanding Hill.
Grid Ref: (A/B) SU590839
                     (C)   SU573838
Maps: OS Landranger Sheet 174
                     OS Explorer Sheet 170
                     OS Pathfinder Sheet 1155 (SU48/58)
How to get there / Parking: (A/B) Moulsford, 3.5 miles south of
    Wallingford, may be reached from the town by taking the
    A329 towards Reading. On entering the village, turn right
    by a telephone box into the recreation ground car park.
    (C) Kingstanding Hill, 4 miles southwest of Wallingford, may
    be reached from the town by taking the Reading road. At the
    Winterbrook Roundabouts first turn right onto the A4130
    towards Didcot then turn left onto the Cholsey road. In Cholsey
    keep straight on towards Blewbury through and out of the
    village to reach the A417 at Kingstanding Hill. Cross this and
    enter a road signposted 'The Downs' where you can park.

Moulsford on the west bank of the Thames near the Goring Gap
and astride the A329, the ancient turnpike road from Wallingford
to Reading, appears always to have been a small place which
history has passed by. The village has a quaint twelfth-century
riverside church with a wooden bellcot next to its ancient manor
house but is perhaps best-known for its picturesque riverside inn,
the 'Beetle and Wedge'. For the walker, however, Moulsford's
principal attraction lies in its being the gateway to an area of the
Downs which combines the large-scale landscape of lofty ridges
and deep coombes typical of the Downs with woodlands more
typical of the nearby Chilterns to produce scenery, the beauty of
which is barely matched anywhere else in the county.

Walks A and B lead you up from the riverside village of Moulsford through the foothills of the Downs to Starveall Farm and Kingstanding Hill where there are fine views of the Downs ahead and back across the Thames Valley towards the Chilterns while Walks A and C explore the ridges and sylvan coombes of the Downs before briefly joining the Ridgeway, turning north over Lowbury Hill, site of a Roman temple and returning by way of the ancient ridgetop droveway known as Aston Tirrold Fairmile.

Walks A and B start by the telephone box in Moulsford and take a gravel track to the cricket pavilion then join path MF12 following a right-hand hedge to a hedge gap at the rear corner of the recreation ground. Go through this then turn left onto path MF3 following a left-hand hedge to a corner of the field. Here go through a hedge gap NOT re-entering the recreation ground but turning right onto fenced path MF6. Where a fence bars your way ahead, bear slightly left through a gap then follow a right-hand hedge straight on for two-thirds of a mile climbing at first then, with fine views of the Downs ahead, following the contours of the ridge above Moulsford Bottom. Where the hedge ends, take a grassy track straight on downhill to the A417.

Turn right onto this road then immediately left onto path MF7, the drive to Starveall Farm, bearing left near the farm to reach the farmhouse. Here turn right and follow a fenced track. Where the track begins to bear left, **Walk A** continues along it (now on path MF4) while **Walk B** turns right over a stile onto path MF4 bearing half right uphill across a field to the corner of a hedge on the skyline. Here take path CS9 keeping left of the hedge and following it (later on path MF13) to a stile leading to a rough road at Kingstanding Hill (CS8). Turn right onto this rejoining Walk A. Now read the last paragraph.

Walk C starts at the A417 crossroads at Kingstanding Hill and takes a rough road (CS8) towards the Downs. After 100 yards, on crossing a row of eight drains, fork left over a stile onto path MF13 following a hedge (later on path CS9). Where the hedge turns left, leave it and take path MF4 straight on descending the field diagonally to cross a stile left of the far corner. Here turn right onto a fenced farm road joining **Walk A**.

Where the right-hand fence ends, **Walks A and C** take path MF4 following the major track bearing left into a green lane. Now take this gravel track straight on for two-thirds of a mile up and over Moulsford Down soon with Unhill Wood to your right and with fine views of the

Downs ahead and across the Thames Valley towards the Chilterns to your left. At the bottom of the next valley where the main track turns sharp left, leave it and take a grassy track straight on keeping left at a fork and entering Harcombe Wood. Now follow this track steeply uphill through the wood to the top of a lower ridge then down again. Where fine views begin to open out across a beautiful sylvan coombe called Cow Common, fork right by a signpost onto a grassy track which soon joins a gravel track. Still on path MF4, follow it straight on for half a mile passing through several outcrops of woodland. Where the main track turns left, leave it and take a grassy path straight on through the woods. On reaching the corner of the garden fence of a gamekeeper's cottage, bear right following the fence past the cottage to a stile. Cross this and turn right onto a stony track passing through gates at the edge of the woods and the Berkshire boundary and now on path ST22 (later AW13) continue, with fine views towards Streatley Warren ahead, to the Ridgeway Path (byway AW10).

Turn right onto this stony road and follow it for nearly half a mile ignoring a branching byway towards Aldworth to your left and the drive to Warren Farm to your right, with wide views opening out to your left towards Watership Down, Cow Down and Nutfield Down and to your right towards the Oxford and Ashendon Hills. At a pronounced left-hand bend leave the Ridgeway and take path AW7 straight on beside a right-hand hedge with panoramic views to your left towards Compton and East Ilsley and ahead towards Harwell and the distant Cotswolds. Where the hedge ends, bear slightly right following a grass crop-break towards Lowbury Hill, site of a Roman temple, later with views to your right towards the Chilterns. On reaching stony byway AW11, join it and follow it over the ridge, keeping right at a fork, re-entering Oxfordshire and (now on AT11/AU6) descending for a quarter mile to reach a crossing green road known as the Aston Tirrold Fairmile.

Turn right onto this ancient droving road (AT13) with a documented width of 132 feet (equivalent to the length of two cricket pitches) and follow it along the ridge for 1.2 miles with fine views to your left towards Didcot Power Station and the Oxford, Ashendon and Sinodun Hills and ahead towards the Chilterns, at one point ignoring a branching track to your left. At the far end of the ridge the green road (now CS8) becomes enclosed between hedges and starts to narrow and descend Cholsey Downs to reach the A417 at Kingstanding Hill where **Walk C** ends and **Walk A** rejoins **Walk B**.

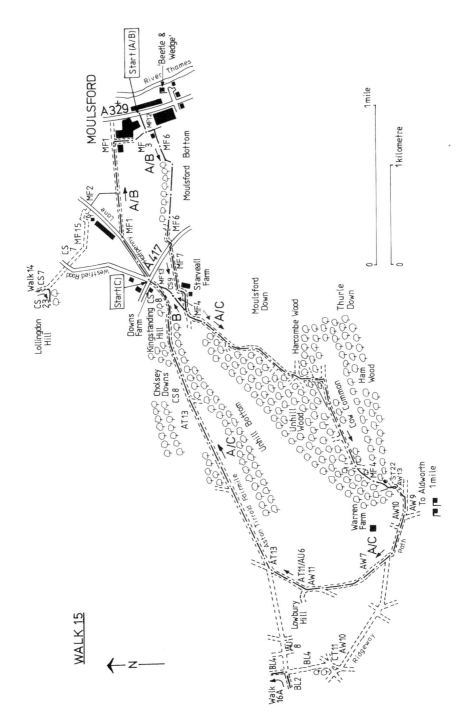

WALK 15

95

Walks A and B now bear slightly right across the A417 and take Halfpenny Lane, the right-hand of two side-roads opposite, straight on for a third of a mile with fine views ahead towards the Chilterns and to your left towards Wittenham Clumps. On nearing a white cottage, fork right onto path MF1 taking a rough track downhill for over half a mile to the edge of Moulsford. Here by the gate to some tennis courts turn right onto path MF3 following a macadam drive then continuing along a lane to a gate and squeeze-stile leading to a playing field. Bear slightly left across this heading just right of a tall tree behind the left-hand hedge to reach a hedge gap leading to the recreation ground then retrace your steps along path MF12 to your starting point.

WALK 16: BLEWBURY

Length of Walk:	(A) 9.1 miles / 14.7 Km
	(B) 6.6 miles / 10.6 Km
Starting Point:	Gates from Church End into Blewbury churchyard.
Grid Ref:	SU532860
Maps:	OS Landranger Sheet 174
	OS Explorer Sheet 170
	OS Pathfinder Sheet 1155 (SU48/58)

How to get there / Parking: Blewbury, 2.5 miles south of Didcot, may be reached from the town by taking the B4016 southwards. On entering Blewbury, at a T-junction turn right onto the A417 and follow it through the village for half a mile. Just past the 'Blewbury Inn' turn right into Westbrook Street. Where the road turns right by Blewbury Hall into Church End, look for a suitable place to park.

Blewbury, on the ancient Celtic Icknield Way at the foot of the Downs, with its maze of narrow lanes and thatched, timbered cottages largely remains the picturesque rural idyll which Kenneth Grahame, author of 'The Wind in the Willows', found it to be on retiring there from being Secretary of the Bank of England in 1910. Blewbury is indeed steeped in history as nearby Blewburton Hill was the site of an Iron Age fort as early as 350BC and in about 870AD King Alfred the Great of Wessex defeated the Danes in a battle near the village and it is from this period that the white-washed thatched wattle and daub walls date which are believed to be a unique feature of Blewbury. The church, though not quite so old, is basically Norman but was subsequently enlarged and has a fifteenth-century tower. The village also has another literary association as the Rev. Morgan Jones, a nineteenth-century parson noted for being a miser, appears as Blewbury Jones in Dickens' 'Out Mutual Friend'. Jones, who was nevertheless respected in Blewbury, is said to have worn the same coat for 42 years and acquired his hat from a scarecrow, yet in his will he left the princely sum of £18,000!

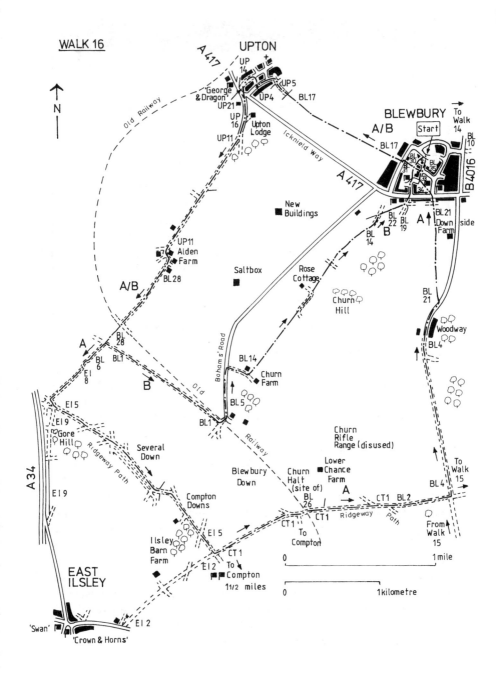

WALK 16

UPTON

BLEWBURY

EAST ILSLEY

Both walks start by leading you through the fascinating village alleyways and along the foot of the Downs to the attractive village of Upton before climbing the Downs to a remote upland valley known as Churn. From here Walk B returns by a direct route over the side of Churn Hill with some fine views out across the Vale, while Walk A climbs to join the Ridgeway Path at Gore Hill and follows the ridgetop towards Compton with views across the Berkshire Downs before recrossing the Churn valley and returning by way of Woodway with more fine views towards the Chilterns and across the Vale.

Both walks start at the gates from Church End into Blewbury churchyard and take path BL30 through these gates into the churchyard and along a paved path passing right of the church tower then continuing between cottage gardens. On reaching a small village green, fork right onto path BL31 following the right-hand edge of the green to cross a footbridge then continuing along an alleyway with one of the wattle and daub walls to your right to reach Westbrook Street. Turn left onto its far pavement then immediately right between safety barriers onto enclosed path BL17 which soon leaves Blewbury behind and gives views in places towards the Downs to your left and Didcot Power Station, then later Wittenham Clumps to your right. Where the hedges and fences end, take a grassy path straight on between arable fields towards Upton with a prominent Victorian red-brick house called Upton Lodge on the hillside above it, eventually crossing a culvert over a stream and continuing to the edge of Upton. Here ignore a crossing path and take path UP5 straight on along a fenced grassy track by a large orchard. At the far end of the orchard disregard branching drives and a path to your left and continue to the end of the village High Street.

Upton, near the junction of the ancient Port Way and Icknield Way, as its name suggests, was once a 'liberty' of Blewbury parish and is a few feet higher than the mother village. Despite this, however, Upton has its own church which is predominantly Norman though with a Saxon doorway and is believed at one time to have been thatched.

Take this road straight on for some 200 yards passing some fine timbered brick cottages and ignoring Church Street to your right. Opposite a bungalow called 'Ryecroft' turn right between safety barriers onto enclosed path UP4 between garden fences. On reaching a concrete road (byway UP14), turn left onto it. Where the road ends, fork left onto narrow fenced path UP21 between gardens to the A417. Bear half left across this into Hollow Way (byway UP16) and follow this road uphill for a quarter-mile. At a fork near the top of the hill keep right following the macadam road (now path UP11) for nearly a mile with fine views opening out over your left shoulder towards the Chilterns and over your right shoulder towards Didcot Power Station and the Oxford Hills, soon crossing the top of the hill where views of the Downs open out ahead.

At Alden Farm ignore a branching farm road and track to your right and follow the concrete road turning sharp left and then right. Now on path BL28, take the concrete road straight on passing right of the remaining farm buildings. Where its concrete surface ends, take a stony track straight on beside a right-hand hedge for half a mile until you reach the crossing over the former Didcot–Newbury–Southampton railway opened in 1882 and closed in 1966. Cross the old railway line and go straight on across a field to a junction of tracks where **Walk A** takes a grassy track (BL6) straight on. Now omit the next two paragraphs.

Walk B turns left onto a green road (BL1) called The Streatley Road and follows it for nearly a mile to a brick bridge over the old railway at Churn. Turn left over this then turn left onto a macadam road (BL5). After a third of a mile turn right onto bridleway BL14 along a concrete road to Churn Farm. Here go past a left-hand barn then turn left and follow the left side of a hedge for nearly a mile with views to your left towards the Harwell Laboratories with their tall brick chimneys, joining a grassy track at one point then leaving it where it turns left towards Rose Cottage and continuing until you reach a crossing track. Here bear slightly right across this to enter an enclosed bridle lane. Where its left-hand fence ends, there is a convenient seat for admiring the superb views which open out at this point across Blewbury towards the Chilterns, Wittenham Clumps, Oxford Hills and distant Cotswolds.

Now continue to follow the sunken way downhill past an old chalkpit soon with fences enclosing it again. After some 350 yards look out for crossing path BL22, onto which you turn right between safety barriers. Now follow its fenced course to a junction of lanes on the edge of Blewbury. Here turn left onto path BL19 to reach the A417. Cross this and take a side road called Nottingham Fee straight on past a timber-framed brick cottage with herringbone brickwork called 'Great Tree' and some fine thatched cottages ignoring a turning to the left. Just past the 'Red Lion' at a right-hand bend take path BL30 straight on between safety barriers then between wattle and daub walls to a culvert leading to a small green. Here keep right at a fork then disregard a crossing path and take a paved path straight on between gardens and through the churchyard retracing your outward route to your starting point.

Walk A follows the track (BL6) to a crossing hedge line marking the Berkshire boundary where it enters a green lane (byway EI8) and follows it uphill for a third of a mile to a crossing concrete road at the top of Gore Hill. Turn left onto this, soon joining the Ridgeway (byway EI5) onto which you bear slightly left. Follow it straight on for one and half miles, soon passing a memorial to a young army officer killed here in an accident with an armoured car in 1947, with wide views to your left towards the Oxford Hills and Chilterns and later to your right towards the Berkshire village of East Ilsley in its valley. Having cross Several Down, you eventually join a concrete road and follow it to the bottom of a dip. Here turn left onto byway CT1, still on the Ridgeway. After two-thirds of a mile, having passed a bridleway to your right, you briefly re-enter Oxfordshire (now on BL26) crossing a bridge over the old railway near the site of the remote Churn Halt. This halt was constructed primarily for the use of soldiers travelling to the former nearby Churn Rifle Range which was set up in the late nineteenth century at the instigation of Robert Loyd Lindsay, Baron Wantage, a local landowner who was awarded two VCs during the Crimean War and was a founder of the Territorial Army.

Back in Berkshire (on byway CT1) continue for half a mile ignoring a branching path and green road to your left. Near the top of a rise fork left onto byway BL2 leaving the Ridgeway and re-entering Oxfordshire. Take this green road gently uphill towards Lowbury Hill for nearly half a mile then turn left onto a crossing green road (BL4). Follow it for a mile later with fine views of the Chilterns to your right to reach the end of a macadam road at Woodway. Take this road straight on for a quarter-mile. Just before a left-hand bend opposite a hedge gap with gates turn left over a stile onto path BL21 with superb views ahead towards Wittenham Clumps, Didcot Power Station, the Oxford Hills and the distant Cotswolds. Now bear right onto a grassy path downhill between arable fields heading towards an electricity pole, the Didcot gasholder and the white Culham Laboratories. Having crossed four fields, join a right-hand fence soon entering a fenced path, crossing a rough lane on the edge of Blewbury and continuing to the A417.

Cross this road and turn left onto a macadam path across a small green. At a crossways bear half right onto enclosed path BL34 descending gently to pass an attractive duckpond and reach the end of Chapel Lane by the Methodist church. Here turn right between safety barriers onto enclosed path BL33 passing a picturesque thatched cottage and another wattle and daub wall to reach the end of another street. Take this straight on ignoring a turning to your right and a branching path to your left. Where the road turns left, bear slightly right between safety barriers onto gravel path BL35 through the churchyard passing right of the church to reach your starting point.

WALK 17: CHARLTON (WANTAGE)

Length of Walk: (A) 10.3 miles / 16.5 Km
(B) 6.8 miles / 11.0 Km
Starting Point: Entrance to The Pound by Charlton Church.
Grid Ref: SU410883
Maps: OS Landranger Sheet 174
OS Explorer Sheet 170
OS Pathfinder Sheet 1155 (SU48/58)
How to get there / Parking: Charlton, 0.8 miles northeast of the centre of Wantage, can be reached from the town centre by taking the A417 towards Reading for 0.7 miles. Just past the 'Lord Nelson', at a double mini-roundabout, turn left onto the road signposted to Charlton Village. After 250 yards at a left-hand bend by Charlton Church turn right into a cul-de-sac called The Pound, then just past the church at a right-hand bend turn left into a cul-de-sac leading to a small car park.
Notes: In summer, path WD4 on Walk A is prone to heavy nettle growth and so it may be preferable to use the East Ginge – West Hendred road.

Charlton, now a suburb of Wantage, was 100 years ago still a village separated by fields from the town. Though historically a hamlet in Wantage parish, Charlton briefly became a separate parish and some of its old farms and cottages, most of which are to be found in the cul-de-sac called The Pound, bear the distinctive features of having once formed part of Baron Wantage's Lockinge Estate.

Both walks soon leave the town behind and lead you over Lark Hill and up to the top of the Downs and the Ridgeway at Betterton Down to reach Baron Wantage's monument at a superb viewpoint. Walk B then redescends the Downs via a long tree-lined avenue to pass through the model estate village of East Lockinge while Walk A continues along the Ridgeway for 2 miles to East Ginge Down before dropping to East Ginge and following Ginge Brook to West Hendred, then turning west through parkland past the estate village of Ardington with its fine eighteenth-century manor house to reach West Lockinge where the routes reunite and lead you back to Charlton.

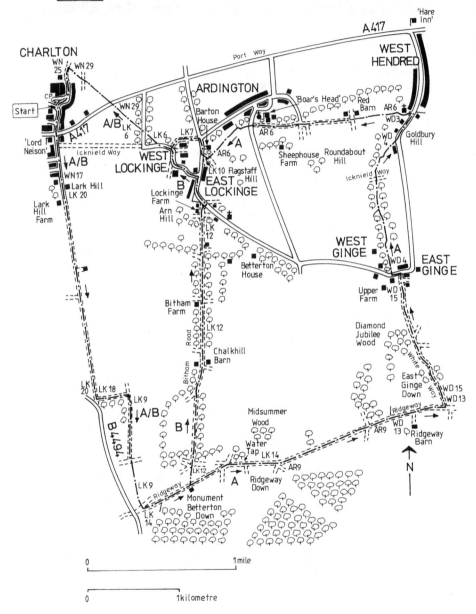

Both walks start from the entrance to The Pound by Charlton Church and turn left into Charlton Village Road following it southwards to its junction with the A417 at the twin mini-roundabouts. Here cross the main road and go straight on up Lark Hill. Where its right-hand footway ends, take path WN17 (later LK20) straight on up a macadam road with fine views opening out towards the Downs ahead, Didcot Power Station and the distant Chilterns to your left and the Oxford Hills behind you. Now keep straight on for 1.3 miles downhill and up again with the macadam surface giving way first to gravel then grassy chalk, eventually reaching the B4494.

Do **NOT** join this road but turn left onto bridleway LK18 taking a grassy track by a right-hand hedged plantation for a quarter mile with fine views towards the Oxford Hills and distant Cotswolds to your left and Chilterns ahead. On reaching crossing bridleway LK9, turn right onto it and follow this old green road for nearly half a mile to a crossing track and fenceline. Here bear slightly right through a bridlegate then go straight on uphill crossing a slight combe then climbing to a bridlegate at the left-hand end of a hedge on the skyline. Go through this and cross a macadam private road then turn left onto the Ridgeway (byway LK14) and follow this ancient green road with superb panoramic views to your left across most of Oxfordshire and part of Buckinghamshire ranging from the Cotswolds to the Chilterns until you reach the monument to Robert Loyd Lindsay, Baron Wantage VC KCB, a local landowner and hero of the Crimean War who was involved in the founding of the Territorial Army, the British Red Cross Society and Reading University. **Walk A** now continues along the Ridgeway omitting the next two paragraphs.

Walk B now turns left onto signposted path LK12 passing through a wide gap in a sporadic belt of small trees and bushes and continuing to a junction of farm roads. Here pass just right of a bend in a macadam road and go straight on through a gap in a tree belt ignoring a branching bridleway to your left and taking a grassy track beside a right-hand tree belt straight on for half a mile to reach a bend in a macadam farm road called Bitham Road. Take this road straight on for 1.2 miles passing Chalkhill Barn where you ignore a turning to your right, then following an avenue of chestnut trees past Bitham Farm where you disregard turnings to right and left and eventually entering parkland used as horse paddocks by a Victorian Neo-Tudor lodge. On reaching Lockinge Farm with a fine long thatched wooden barn, bear right to join the public road through East Lockinge, a model estate village whose cottages were largely built or refurbished by Baron Wantage in the 1860s with a much-extended Norman church set in parkland near the site of the Baron's large Victorian manor house demolished in 1947.

Turn left onto the roadside footway and follow it through this fascinating village with fine views across its beautiful park, passing the ornate war memorial and a number of Victorian estate cottages. At a road junction turn left onto the West Lockinge road and follow it into and through this scattered hamlet rounding a sharp right-hand, then a left-hand bend where you join the ancient Icknield Way, rejoin Walk A and enter another avenue of chestnut trees. Now read the last paragraph.

Walk A continues on the Ridgeway (LK14 at first) for a further 1.8 miles, ignoring a bridleway merging from the left by a copse, passing a drinking water tap and later disregarding a branching green road to your right where you bear slightly left (now on byway AR9) and views across Berkshire begin to open out to your right. By a second left-hand copse ignore a crossing bridleway then soon after disregard a branching bridleway to your left. Now on byway WD13 continue over East Ginge Down with more superb panoramic views with Harwell Laboratory with its red-brick chimneys in the foreground. Some 700 yards beyond the branching bridleway turn left through an iron gate onto White Way (WD15), a grassy track across a field to a gap between two copses to pass through green gates. Now continue downhill between the copses and across a field to gates by Diamond Jubilee Wood to your left. Here ignore a branching track to your right and take a track straight on along the edge of the wood. Where the main track bears away right, leave it and take a green lane straight on downhill along the edge of the wood entering a sunken way and continuing for nearly half a mile until you pass a thatched cottage and reach the village street in East Ginge.

Turn left onto this road. After 100 yards by a red-brick cottage to your left turn right onto enclosed path WD4 along the side of a steep ravine containing Ginge Brook through scrubby woodland to emerge into the corner of a field. Here follow a sunken way straight on along the edge of the field. At the far end of the field go straight on through more scrubby woodland for a quarter mile, at one point disregarding a branching path to your left. Having passed an old iron gate, ignore a hedge gap to your right and continue through scrub to emerge onto a crossing bridleway (part of the ancient Icknield Way). Now follow the outside edge of the wood straight on with views of Goldbury Hill ahead. Near the far end of the field by a pronounced outcrop of woodland, cross the field corner diagonally, heading left of Goldbury Hill and a row of council houses then take a grass path diagonally across some allotments to a low rail-stile. Now take a fenced path straight on to a rail-stile onto a road on the edge of West Hendred.

Turn left onto this road and follow it into the village passing a large house to your left. Just past a thatched cottage turn left into the road to the church then take path WD3 straight on through a lychgate into the churchyard. Here take a paved path passing left of the church (of fourteenth-century appearance but believed to be older) to reach a kissing-gate and footbridge then go straight on across a field to cross a stile and bridge over Ginge Brook. Now take path AR6 bearing half left through a belt of trees. Where the path forks, bear right. On entering a field, bear half left along a grassy path between arable fields over a slight rise towards the inappropriately-named Red Barn, gradually bearing left to pass left of the buildings. By the buildings at a junction of farm roads take a macadam road straight on for over a third of a mile. Where it turns right towards Ardington, leave it and go straight on over a stile by a New Zealand (barbed-wire) gate then take a grassy track straight on beside a right-hand fence and a belt of trees, at one point ignoring a gate and footbridge to your right. Where the tree-belt ends and the fence bears right, fine views open out to your right towards Ardington village.

Ardington, which, like East Lockinge, is an estate village, has an imposing manor house known as Ardington House built in about 1720 for Edward Clarke, whose family held the manor for about 500 years, by the Strong family, who had worked for Vanbrugh on Blenheim Palace and incorporated some of Vanbrugh's ideas in their design noted for its spectacular staircase. In the early nineteenth century the house was acquired by Robert Vernon (1774–1849), a poor horse-trader who had become rich during the Napoleonic Wars and acquired a taste for fine paintings. Shortly before his death he donated a collection of 157 paintings he had amassed at Ardington to the National Gallery. The nearby church, containing memorials to Robert Vernon and the Clarke family and the burial place in 1901 of Baron Wantage, is of twelfth-century origin but was heavily restored and given its present tower and spire in 1847.

Take the track straight on soon with a fence and tree-belt to your right. On reaching a road, cross it and a stile by a New Zealand gate opposite then (still on path AR6) follow a right-hand fence straight on to cross a stile. Now bear half left heading for a tall Scots pine and ash trees left of Barton House, a large Victorian house ahead, ignoring a stile to your right and joining a distinct grass path. Pass left of these trees and continue to a gate and stile under a tall chestnut tree. Here take fenced path LK10 bearing right to join a macadam drive onto which you bear slightly right crossing a stone bridge and continuing to a stile left of an iron gate onto a road on the edge of East Lockinge. Turn right onto this road and at a junction turn left onto bridleway LK7 following a fenced track straight on, ignoring a branching path to your left then eventually bearing left to reach a bend in a road at West Lockinge. Turn right onto this road joining the Icknield Way, rejoining Walk B and entering an avenue of chestnut trees.

Walks A and B now follow an unmade path along the top of the right-hand bank of the road for some 200 yards to a stile in the right hand fence. Turn right over this onto path LK6 bearing half left across two paddocks to a stile in a belt of trees leading to a road. Cross the road and go through a hedge gap opposite then bear half right across two fields heading towards the left-hand-most and most prominent pylon in the nearest of several powerlines (on path WN29 in the second field) to reach a culvert leading to the A417. Cross this road and go through a fence gap opposite then bear slightly left across a field passing just left of the twin-poled pylon to cross a rail-stile in the next fence. Now keep straight on to a gap in the next fence where you cross a track and go through a fence gap by a disused gate opposite then bear half right across the next field to a stile in the far corner leading into a green lane (WN25). Turn left into this and follow it to the end of The Pound in Charlton then continue along this road passing a fine Victorian farmhouse to reach your starting point.

WALK 18: WANTAGE

Length of Walk: (A) 10.8 miles / 17.4 Km
(B) 5.8 miles / 9.4 Km
Starting Point: 'Shears' public house at the junction of
Mill Street and Limborough Road, Wantage.
Grid Ref: SU397880
Maps: OS Landranger Sheet 174
OS Explorer Sheet 170
OS Pathfinder Sheet 1154 (SU28/38)
How to get there / Parking: From the Market Place in the centre
of Wantage take Mill Street northwestwards then turn right
into Limborough Road where there is a public car park on
your right.

Wantage, a traditional English market town at the foot of the
Downs, is perhaps best known as the birthplace of King Alfred the
Great of Wessex (849AD–899AD) whose statue has stood in the
Market Place since 1877. Legend has it that after his flight from the
invading Danes in 878 he allowed a Somerset peasant's cakes to
burn, but Alfred earned his title of 'the Great' by organising a
counter-offensive which comprehensively defeated Guthram's
Danes at Edington (Wilts.) in 879 and led to the Peace of Wedmore
establishing Watling Street as their mutual boundary. Having
removed the Danish threat, Alfred then capitalised on the peace by
reviving education and the rule of the law, but 100 years after his
death the bellicose Danes were again attacking Wessex and burnt
Wantage down in 1001. Another famous son of Wantage was the
Victorian architect George Street who restored the town's fine
largely thirteenth-century church and later went on to design
London's Law Courts, but in addition to the church, Wantage has
many fine seventeenth to nineteenth century houses which give
the town its special character.

Both walks explore the beautiful foothills of the Downs first
taking you to the picturesque racehorse-training village of
Letcombe Regis where King John is said to have had a hunting
lodge from which the village's royal appendage derives. Walk A

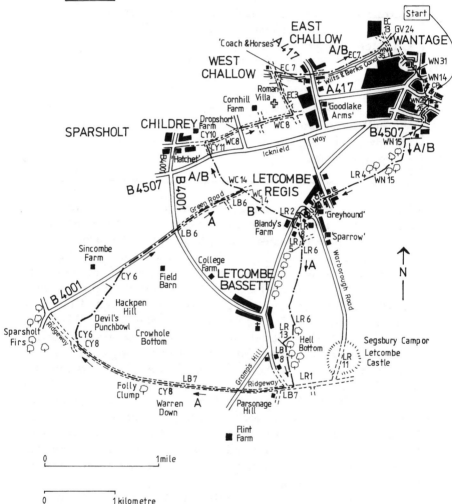

then leads you on uphill past Letcombe Bassett to the Ridgeway near the Iron Age hill fort known as Segsbury Camp or Letcombe Castle before following this ancient road with its spectacular scenery along the crest of the Downs for two miles to Hackpen Hill and the Devil's Punchbowl. Having descended the escarpment and rejoined Walk B, both walks continue with fine views, passing Childrey and the site of a Roman villa before joining the towpath of the former Wilts. and Berks. Canal and following it through East Challow back to Wantage.

Both walks start from the 'Shears' public house at the junction of Mill Street and Limborough Road, Wantage and take Mill Street northwestwards crossing a bridge over Letcombe Brook. Now turn immediately left onto path WN28, an alleyway through a flour-mill once driven by the brook, joining its bank. On reaching a bridge, turn left onto path WN26 crossing the bridge and continuing along an alleyway. By some steps into the churchyard turn right to join Priory Road then continue past some Victorian terraced cottages. Ignore Locks Lane to your right and bear left then right to reach Portway (the modern B4507 and part of the Ancient British Icknield Way) by a stone-built Victorian school.

Bear slightly right across this road and take enclosed path WN15 straight on, eventually emerging by a cottage at the edge of a fenced playing field. Here fork right onto a macadam path beside the playing field fence then turn left beside a row of tall poplars, soon leaving the playing field behind and following an enclosed macadam path. After nearly half a mile you pass between safety barriers and take the more open path LR4 straight on with views of the Downs ahead and to your right to reach the end of a road on the edge of Letcombe Regis. Take this road straight on to a staggered crossroads then continue along the priority road towards Letcombe Bassett following its winding course for some 340 yards past the 'Greyhound' to a crossroads by the church, which is of Norman origin but largely rebuilt in the fifteenth century. Here take the road to Letcombe Laboratory straight on, forking right by an ornamental thatched brick-and-flint lodge. Where the road ends at some gates, turn right onto fenced macadam path LR8. Follow it to Bassett Road then turn left soon passing an attractive lake in the laboratory grounds to your left. **Walk A** now keeps straight on omitting the next paragraph.

After about 120 yards by a tall chestnut tree to your right **Walk B** turns right between safety rails and takes fenced path LR2 for some 270 yards to enter a right-hand field. Here follow the left-hand hedge straight on, soon with a right-hand hedge and fence enclosing the path again. On crossing a stile, follow the bottom of a steep bank and a sporadic hedge straight on with views of the Downs to your left. At the far end of the field (now on path WC14) turn right through a hedge gap and over a stile then turn left onto a grassy track called Green Road (LB6). On reaching the end of an earth bank to your right, fork right onto the continuation of path WC14 rejoining Walk A and following the bottom of the bank. Now omit the next four paragraphs.

Walk A follows Bassett Road for some 250 yards. Just past a brick and timber cottage by the entrance to Blandy's Farmyard, turn left onto path LR5 taking a green lane over a bridge to a gate and stile into a field. Here follow the left-hand fence uphill to a gate and stile into a green lane (bridleway LR6). Turn right into this lane with a fine view of the Downs opening out ahead. Ignore a branching path to your right and go straight on through a gate into a field then follow a right-hand fence straight on towards the Downs with Letcombe Bassett coming into view in a hollow to your right.

Letcombe Bassett, another racehorse-training village with a Norman church, picturesque timber-framed thatched cottages and watercress beds, is a place with literary connections, as Thomas Hardy stayed here and used Letcombe Bassett as the model for Cresscombe in his 'Jude the Obscure' while Jonathan Swift stayed at the Rectory in 1714 and was visited by Alexander Pope. At the far end of the field cross a stile by a gate and take a fenced path straight on then at the far end of the left-hand field turn right over a stile by a disused gate onto path LR13 turning left and following a left-hand hedge then the edge of a wood in Hell Bottom to a stile into the wood. Take an obvious path straight on through the wood to a stile into a field. Now turn left onto path LB8 following the edge of the wood downhill and up again through three fields with wide views opening out behind you across the Vale of the White Horse and Thames Valley towards Badbury Hill, Folly Hill and the distant Cotswolds. By the top corner of the wood cross a stile and go straight on uphill with Segsbury Camp or Letcombe Castle, an Iron Age hill fort coming into view to your left and views towards the Oxford Hills and distant Chilterns opening out over your left shoulder, then at the top of the field cross a stile onto the ancient Ridgeway.

If wishing to visit Segsbury Camp, turn left onto this green road (LR1) later turning left onto another green road (LR11) which crosses the hill fort. Otherwise, turn right onto the green road (LB7) with fine views to your right as before and to your left across the Downs towards Walbury Hill and Inkpen Hill near Hungerford. After half a mile cross a road up from Letcombe Bassett known as Gramp's Hill and keep straight on soon with more superb views ahead and to your right including Hackpen Hill and a spectacular coombe called Crowhole Bottom which culminates in the Devil's Punchbowl. Now continue for a further 1.5 miles (later on CY8).

Near the far end of the coombe turn right over a ladder-stile onto path CY6 going straight across a field with fine views to your right towards Letcombe Bassett and the distant Chilterns to a stile leading to the coombe. Here continue across the top of coombe to join a left-hand fence and follow it to a rail-stile above the steepest part known as the Devil's Punchbowl. Turn left over this stile and go straight across a field to another rail-stile at the top of Hackpen Hill where there are superb views ahead across the Vale of the White Horse and Thames Valley. Now bear half right across the next field to a rail-stile in the next fence then continue, heading just right of Childrey in the valley below to cross ladder and rail stiles. Here bear slightly right downhill to cross a stile in the bottom fence of the field and descend some steps onto the B4001. Turn right onto this road and follow it for half a mile, soon with views of the Downs to your right. At a junction leave the B4001 and take a grassy track called Green Road (LB6) straight on with fine views to your left across the Vale, ahead towards Didcot Power Station and the distant Chilterns and to your right towards the Letcombes and Downs. Eventually you enter a green lane and follow it ignoring a branching bridleway to your right. On emerging from this lane, by the end of a low bank to your left, turn sharp left onto path WC14 rejoining Walk B and following the bottom of the bank.

Walks A and B now follow this bank for nearly half a mile with views of Hackpen Hill to your left, to reach the B4507 (Icknield Way). Cross this and take path CY11 straight on through a gate onto a fenced track leading you downhill to meet macadam bridleway CY10 near the edge of Childrey with its attractive duckpond. Turn right onto this bridleway and follow it straight on for three-quarters of a mile, soon becoming bridleway WC8 then crossing the road to West Challow, a tiny village with a Norman church with the oldest bell in England bearing the maker's name thought to date from 1282, and continuing past Cornhill Farm and the unmarked site of a Roman Villa. On nearing East Challow, turn left into a gravel lane called Cornhill Lane (EC3) signposted 'Recreation ground and car park'. Where the gravel track turns right into the recreation ground, leave it and take the green lane straight on downhill for a quarter mile ignoring a crossing path and eventually crossing a wooden bridge over the former Wilts. and Berks. Canal. Completed in 1810, this canal, which linked the Thames and Abingdon to Swindon and the Avon, could not compete with the Great Western Railway built some 30 years later and eventually closed in 1914, since when long stretches of it have dried out or been filled in.

Turn right onto the old canal towpath (EC7) then, where the canal has been filled in, continue along a fenced path to the A417 at East Challow. Cross this road carefully (beware of the blind bend to your left!) and take a macadam lane (still path EC7) straight on. Just before a house called 'The Granary' fork right onto a fenced path soon with the canal resuming to your right and follow the old towpath for over half a mile. Where the canal has been filled in again, take the gravel path straight on to a gate and stile then turn right onto path GV24 following a macadam lane which soon bears right and climbs (now as WN35) to reach a fence gap into a housing estate. Here turn left onto a macadam path and follow it, ignoring a branching path to your right, to the frame of an old kissing-gate. Now take a concrete road straight on, soon bearing right to reach an estate road. At a T-junction turn left then by some garages bear right and ignore a turning to your left. At a further right-hand bend just past a sign for Stockham Way turn left between bollards onto concrete path WN31 and follow it to Denchworth Road. Cross this road and turn right onto its far pavement then turn left into Belmont, immediately forking right onto path WN14 and taking this macadam alleyway gently downhill ignoring branching paths to right and left. On reaching a road, cross it and take a macadam path straight on to Mill Street virtually opposite the 'Shears'.

Length of Walk: 6.8 miles / 10.9 Km
Starting Point: Entrance to Uffington Village Hall car park.
Grid Ref: SU307894
Maps: OS Landranger Sheet 174
OS Explorer Sheet 170
OS Pathfinder Sheet 1154 (SU28/38)
How to get there / Parking: Uffington, 4 miles south of
Faringdon, may be reached from the junctions of the A417
and A420 (Faringdon Bypass) by taking the A420 towards
Swindon and Bristol and turning left onto the Little Coxwell
and Fernham road. In Fernham turn left onto the B4508
towards Wantage. On leaving the village, at a sharp left-
hand bend fork right onto the Uffington road. In Uffington
turn left towards Kingston Lisle then pass the turning for
Whitehorse Hill and Ashbury and look out for the village
hall car park on your right.

Uffington at the foot of the Downs is best known for the White
Horse on the side of Whitehorse Hill generally believed to be the
oldest of the fifteen such horses in England and to be about
2,000 years old, although some think it only dates from Saxon
times. Its prominence as a local landmark has resulted in the Ock
valley below becoming known as the Vale of the White Horse and
in 1974 this also became the name of the local district council.
Whitehorse Hill, which at 856ft is the highest point in Oxfordshire,
has even older historical significance as it is capped by a large
well-preserved hillfort known as Uffington Castle enclosing some
eight acres of land which is believed to date from 500BC, while
Dragon Hill to the north is variously said to be the site of St.
George's slaying of the dragon or the burial place of Uther
Pendragon, father of King Arthur. The village of Uffington,
however, is also not without historical interest as in 1822 it was the
birthplace of Thomas Hughes, author of 'Tom Brown's Schooldays',
whose grandfather was Vicar of Uffington from 1816 to 1833.
Hughes, who apart from being an author was a County Court judge

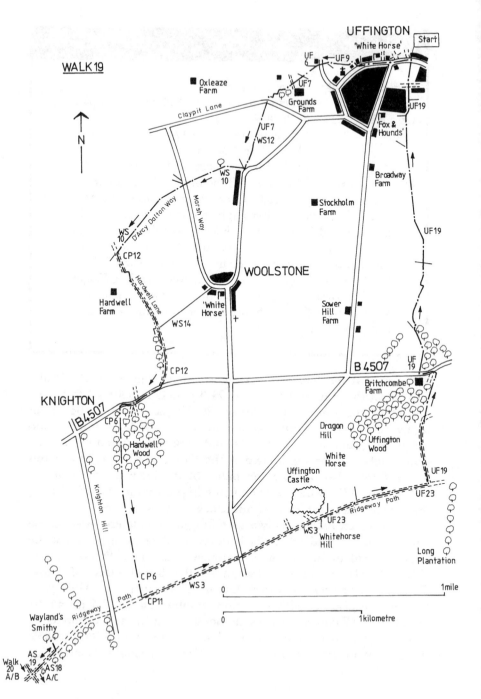

WALK 19

UFFINGTON

Start

'White Horse'

UF 6 UF 9

UF 7

Oxleaze Farm

Grounds Farm

Claypit Lane

N

UF 7

WS12

'Fox & Hounds'

UF19

WS 10

Broadway Farm

D'Arcy Dalton Way

Marsh Way

WS 10

UF19

Stockholm Farm

CP12

Hardwell Lane

WOOLSTONE

Hardwell Farm

'White Horse'

WS14

Sower Hill Farm

CP12

B 4507

UF 19

KNIGHTON

B4507

Britchcombe Farm

CP6

Hardwell Wood

Dragon Hill

Uffington Wood

White Horse

Knighton Hill

Uffington Castle

UF19

UF23

Ridgeway Path

UF23

WS3

Whitehorse Hill

Long Plantation

CP6

WS3

Path

Ridgeway

CP11

Wayland's Smithy

0   1mile

0   1kilometre

Walk 20 A/B

AS 19

AS18

A/C

116

and one-time MP for Lambeth and Frome, set Tom Brown's early childhood in the village depicting local village life in vivid terms. Uffington has a Tom Brown's School Museum and there is a memorial to Hughes in the fine thirteenth-century parish church with its unusual octagonal tower whose spire was destroyed by lightning in 1740.

The walk, which includes some superb panoramic views, first leads you through Uffington and past the picturesque village of Woolstone to the foot of the Downs before climbing through woodland to reach the Ridgeway at the top of Knighton Hill. You then follow this ancient track over Whitehorse Hill before descending by way of Britchcombe Farm in its wooded coombe to Uffington.

Starting from the entrance to Uffington Village Hall car park, turn left and take Broad Street back towards the village centre passing the 'White Horse'. On reaching a filling station, turn right onto path UF9 passing right of the garage buildings then bearing slightly left to a gate and stile at the back left-hand corner of its yard where there is a fine view of Uffington Church to your left. Now follow a left-hand fence straight on to the far end of the field. Here ignore a stile to your left and go straight on over a footbridge then bear slightly left under a willow tree to reach Fernham Road. Cross this and take path UF6 through a hedge gap opposite. Now bear slightly left passing left of a thatched cottage then following its wall to a stile into a field. Here take path UF7 straight on across the field heading for the middle of a copse just right of a large grey barn at Grounds Farm and crossing a track at one point. On reaching the copse, bear slightly right along its outside edge then just past its far end turn left over a stile and footbridge. Now cross Claypit Lane and a stile opposite and go straight on across a field with a fine view of Whitehorse Hill to your left heading for the middle of a row of willow trees. Here go through a gate and cross a culvert then turn left onto path WS12 crossing a stile and footbridge then following a right-hand hedge to a gate leading to a road on the edge of Woolstone.

Do NOT join this road but turn right over a footbridge onto fenced path WS10 along the bank of a stream to another footbridge. Here go straight on keeping right of a line of willows to cross two stiles into a field then follow a right-hand hedge straight on past a copse to cross a rail-stile and two footbridges. Now bear half left and follow a left-hand hedge to cross a stile by gates onto Marsh Way. Cross this road and bear half left (still on path WS10) joining the D'Arcy Dalton Way and following a left-hand hedge and ditch to cross a rail-stile and footbridge at the far end of the field. Now bear half left across the next field to cross two stiles at its far corner. Here, leaving the D'Arcy Dalton Way, turn left into Hardwell Lane (CP12), a fenced track towards the Downs, soon turning left over a bridge then right into a narrow green lane. Now follow this for half a mile gently climbing to reach the B4507, part of the ancient Icknield Way.

Turn right onto this road and follow it for 350 yards with fine views across the Vale to your right. As you pass Hardwell Wood to your left, look out for path CP6 into the wood just before a left-hand bend. Turn left onto this, crossing a stile and following a sunken way uphill to cross another stile. Now take a path between hedges straight on, eventually emerging into a field with fine views to your left towards Whitehorse Hill and the distant Oxford Hills and to your right towards Swindon. Here keep straight on over the ridge heading just right of a distant radio mast to reach the Ridgeway. Turn left onto this ancient green road (CP11, later WS3 then UF23) and follow it for 1.4 miles crossing a rough road then climbing Whitehorse Hill with its spectacular panoramic views. At the top of the ridge superb views open out towards Didcot Power Station and the distant Chilterns and to your right towards Inkpen Hill and Walbury Hill south of Hungerford.

Some 200 yards short of a tree-belt called Long Plantation, where a left-hand fence resumes, turn left onto path UF19, a grassy track with fine views across the Vale opening out ahead. By a corner of Uffington Wood cross a stile by a gate and leave the track following the outside edge of the wood steeply downhill through two fields. Near the bottom end of the second field turn left over a stile and descend steeply through woodland to reach a bend in the B4507 (Icknield Way) near Britchcombe Farm. Turn left onto this road then opposite a wooden barn at the farm turn right through a hedge gap (still on path UF19) and bear slightly right following the outside edge of a wood through two fields. At the far end of the second field turn right over a culvert and stile then turn left and follow a left-hand hedge through two fields with views to your right towards Fawler. Some 40 yards short of the far end of the second field turn left over a concealed footbridge and stile then turn right and follow a right-hand hedge to a corner of the field. Here go through a hedge gap then ignore a footbridge to your right and turn left over a stile then right and follow a right-hand fence to cross two stiles in the next hedge where Uffington comes into view ahead. Here bear slightly left across the next field heading just left of Uffington Church to cross a stile. Now follow a right-hand hedge straight on through five fields with fine views of Whitehorse Hill behind you, to reach the edge of Uffington village. At the far end of the fifth field turn right over a stile then left and follow a left-hand hedge to a gate in a corner of the field. Now go straight on through the gate and along a fenced path to a rough road then keep straight on through a hedge gap and across a recreation ground to reach the village hall car park.

WALK 20: ASHBURY

Length of Walk: (A) 7.0 miles / 11.3 Km
  (B) 3.1 miles / 5.0 Km
  (C) 5.1 miles / 8.3 Km
  (Detour to Wayland's Smithy) + 0.4 miles / 0.6 Km
Starting Point: Car park on the Ridgeway at Ashbury Folly.
Grid Ref: SU273843
Maps: OS Landranger Sheet 174
  OS Explorer Sheet 170
  OS Pathfinder Sheet 1154 (SU28/38)
How to get there / Parking: Ashbury Folly, 8 miles southwest of Wantage, may be reached from the town by taking the B4507 to Ashbury then turning left onto the B4000 and following it up Ashbury Hill to a small car park on the Ridgeway signposted 'Wayland's Smithy'.

Ashbury, on the ancient Icknield Way at the foot of the Downs and since 1974 in the extreme southwest corner of Oxfordshire near its borders with Wiltshire and Berkshire, is a picturesque village with a fifteenth-century manor house and sixteenth-century cottages. Its church, which is of Norman origin but with a later tower and chancel and a very early brass dating from 1360, was in 1777 the scene of one of the first Sunday schools in England set up by the Reverend Thomas Stock, who is said to have given the idea to Robert Raikes, who is normally credited as being the founder of the Sunday school movement. Above the village on the Downs near the ancient Ridgeway is Wayland's Smithy, an extremely well-preserved Neolithic chambered long barrow believed to date from about 3400BC surrounded by a ring of trees. Its name is however of Saxon origin deriving from a mythical smith called Weland. Legend has it that if a horse, which has lost a shoe, is left tethered at the Smithy for ten minutes, a silver coin is left and the rider whistles three times, Weland will shoe the horse and take the silver in payment.

All three walks start on the Ridgeway above Ashbury and have a short optional detour to Wayland's Smithy. While Walks A and B also descend the Downs to visit Ashbury with superb views out across the Vale of the White Horse, Walks A and C explore the hills beyond the Ridgeway crossing Weathercock Hill to skirt Ashdown Park with its seventeenth-century National Trust house and an Iron Age hill fort known as Alfred's Castle before returning to Ashbury Folly.

Walks A and B start from the car park at Ashbury Folly at the junction of the B4000 and the Ridgeway and take the Ridgeway (AS18) southwestwards for a quarter mile. At a signposted crossways turn right through a hedge gap onto path AS2 following a sporadic right-hand hedge then a fence with superb views opening out to your left towards Bishopstone Downs and Swindon and later ahead across the Vale of the White Horse and the Thames Valley towards the distant Cotswolds. After a quarter mile the right-hand fence ends and a left-hand fence begins and you start to descend towards Ashbury Church soon with a sporadic hedge to your right. At a T-junction with a crossing bridleway (AS1) turn left onto it soon with a fence to your left. On reaching a macadam path, turn right onto it and follow it downhill past the church keeping right at a fork and continuing downhill to a T-junction by the 'Rose and Crown'.

Here turn left into High Street. By the war memorial fork right into Chapel Road (signposted to Shrivenham) bearing right by Manor Farm where you glimpse the fifteenth-century manor. On nearing a T-junction with the B4000, keep left at a fork then cross the main road and take macadamed bridleway AS30 straight on between bollards, soon descending to reach an attractive duckpond then climbing again to a T-junction in Kingstone Winslow.

Here turn right onto a road passing Kingstone Farm. On nearing the B4507, keep right at a fork then cross the B4507 and a stile opposite onto path AS8 following a right-hand hedge along the bottom of a steep downland bank rich in wildflowers known as Winslow Bank. On emerging into a field, follow the bottom of the steep bank soon with a wire fence to your right and continue for 250 yards to two stiles. Now follow the bottom edge of a belt of beech trees straight on, gradually climbing the side of Odstone Coombe. At the far end of the tree belt join a left-hand fence with superb views to your left across the Vale of the White Horse and Thames Valley towards the Cotswolds and behind over Swindon. At the top of a steep chalky slope bear half right across a field to a New Zealand (barbed-wire) gate in a fence ahead. Go through this and turn right into sunken way AS19 up Odstone Hill, soon joining a chalk road with more fine views to your right, to reach a crossways with the Ridgeway (AS18) where Wayland's Smithy is some 300 yards to your left and **Walk B** turns right onto the Ridgeway and follows it for two-thirds of a mile to your starting point. For **Walk A** now omit the next paragraph.

Walk C starts from the car park at Ashbury Folly at the junction of the B4000 and the Ridgeway and takes the Ridgeway (AS18) towards Wayland's Smith for two-thirds of a mile passing through a belt of trees and continuing to a major crossways where Wayland's Smithy is some 300 yards ahead and **Walk C** turns right to join Walk A.

Walks A and C now take a wide chalky lane (AS19) straight on for over half a mile. Just past a storm-ravaged beech copse called Down Folly at a crossways take bridleway AS25 straight on between plantations into a field where there are fine views to your left towards Woolstone Down, to your right towards Bishopstone Downs and ahead into the Lambourn valley. Here leave the track and go straight on across the field dropping to join a grass crop break at a bend in it at the far end of a sporadic row of hawthorn bushes. Now take this crop break straight on for a quarter mile until you reach an old four-way signpost. Here bear half right onto path AS36 leaving the crop break and heading for a point on the skyline midway between a clump of trees on Weathercock Hill and the left-hand end of a belt of woodland at Crowberry Tump where those with excellent eyesight may spot a marker post. By the marker post, where there are fine views of Woolstone Down behind you and towards the Lambourn valley to your left, cross a track and bear half left heading right of the clump of trees by the weathercock on Weathercock Hill to reach the corner of a fence. Here keep straight on towards the left-hand end of Upper Wood in the valley ahead with Ashdown House soon coming into view to your right.

Ashdown House, built in about 1665 by William, first Earl of Craven in the Dutch style for Elizabeth, Queen of Bohemia and daughter of James I, is an unusually tall, narrow house with a mansard roof capped by a viewing platform and a cupola with a golden ball. However Elizabeth died before she could move into this house which Pevsner described as 'the perfect doll's house'.

Now skirt the left-hand edge of a deep coombe and gradually bear right towards Ashdown Farm hidden in trees left of Ashdown House,

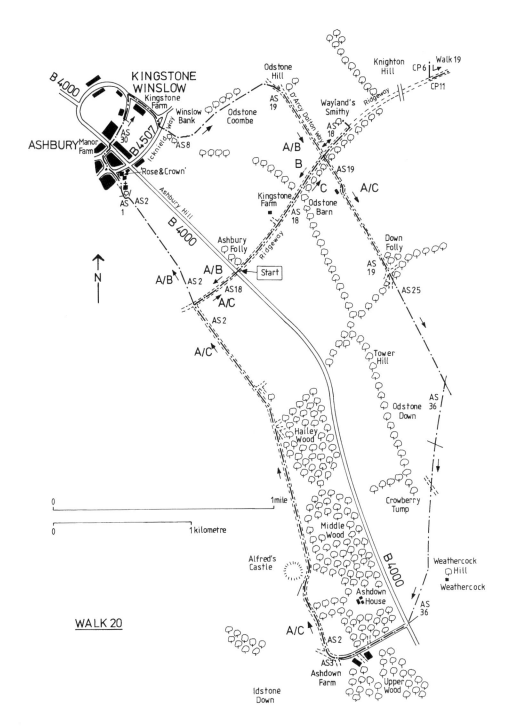

WALK 20

0 ————————————————— 1 mile

0 ————————————— 1 kilometre

123

eventually dropping to cross hurdles and a stile at a road junction. Here cross the B4000 and take a side road straight on past a private entrance to Ashdown House, some fine lime trees and the red-brick Jacobean Ashdown Farm. Just past the farm the road loses its macadam surface then, where it forks, take AS3 straight on through a gate. On passing through a second gate, fork right and take path AS2 along a grassy track beside a right-hand hedge uphill past the back of Ashdown House to cross a stile by a gate near the Iron Age hill fort known as Alfred's Castle. Continue to another gate and stile then bear half left and follow an ill-defined grassy track passing left of an outcrop of Middle Wood then later joining a left-hand fence and following it for a third of a mile to a gate, horse-jump and stile by a corner of Hailey Wood. Here ignore branching tracks to your right and take a grassy track straight on towards a clump of chestnut trees where you bear slightly left and continue for over half a mile, eventually joining a right-hand hedge and following it to a hedge gap onto the Ridgeway (AS18). Now turn right onto this for your starting point.

WALK 21:   GREAT COXWELL
(BADBURY CLUMP PICNIC AREA)

Length of Walk: 5.9 miles / 9.5 Km
Starting Point: Entrance to Badbury Clump Picnic Area.
Grid Ref: SU262945
Maps: OS Landranger Sheet 163
OS Explorer Sheet 170
OS Pathfinder Sheet 1135 (SU29/39)
How to get there / Parking: Badbury Clump Picnic Area,
1.8 miles southwest of the centre of Faringdon, may be
reached from the town by taking the B4019 towards
Highworth. A quarter mile beyond the Great Coxwell
turn fork right into the unmarked picnic area at Badbury
Clump.

Great Coxwell on the slopes of Badbury Hill with its fine views
across the Ock valley or Vale of the White Horse towards White
Horse Hill is probably best known for its magnificent
thirteenth-century tithe barn. This barn known as Great Barn was
built by Cistercian monks from Beaulieu Abbey (Hants.) to house
the parish tithes (a tax in kind of one-tenth of agricultural
produce exacted from the ninth century onwards to pay for parish
priests) which the Abbey received from local farmers after the
Manor was given to it by King John in 1204. Donated to the
National Trust in 1956, this Cotswold-stone barn, which is over
150 feet long, is interesting both for its timber-framed interior
construction and its sheer age as few agricultural buildings of this
period have survived.

This walk, which is almost entirely on National Trust land,
explores the range of hills between Faringdon and the Wiltshire
border with its pleasant woods and wealth of fine views, leading
you first down from Badbury Hill into Great Coxwell where you
pass Great Barn before turning west for the ancient estate village of
Coleshill on the Wiltshire border and returning along the other
side of the ridge to the wooded north side of Badbury Hill.

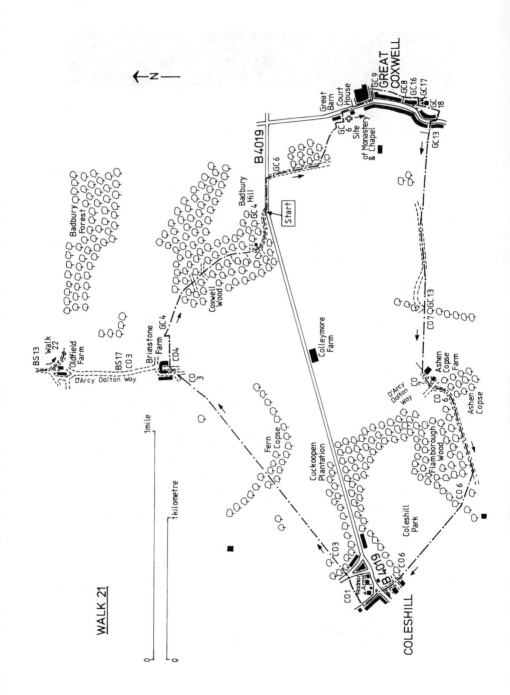

WALK 21

Starting from the entrance to Badbury Clump Picnic Area, take the B4019 towards Faringdon for over 200 yards with fine views through the hedges in places to your left across the Thames Valley towards Wytham Hill and the Cotswolds and to your right towards the Downs. Just before a crossroads sign turn right over a stile by a gate onto path GC6 taking a grass track between fields downhill with fine views of the Downs ahead, joining a left-hand fence and following it past a plantation. Soon after mature woodland begins to your left, look out for a stile into it. Cross this and bear half right across the bottom corner of the wood to a footbridge and stile into a field then turn left and follow a left-hand hedge, later a fence towards Great Barn. At a field corner near the barn bear right and follow a left-hand hedge to a gate and stile in it then turn left over the stile and take a gravel drive passing right of the barn to reach a village street in Great Coxwell.

Turn right onto this road into the village then take the second turning left. After passing a right-hand cottage abutting the road, turn right onto path GC9 along a rough lane called Dark Lane into a field where there is a fine view towards Whitehorse HIll ahead. Now follow the right-hand edge of the field straight on joining macadam path GC8. Where it turns left across the field, take path GC16 straight on along the field edge. After 100 yards turn right through a bollarded gap in the churchyard wall onto grassy path GC17 passing right of the twelfth-century church to reach a stone path leading to the church door. Cross this and turn left onto grassy path GC18 following the right-hand edge of the churchyard past the fifteenth-century church tower to a stile into a field. Here continue beside a right-hand fence and hedge to a corner then turn right and follow a right-hand stone wall to a gate and stile onto a village street, onto which you turn right.

After 40 yards, just past Wrekin Cottage, turn left onto path GC13 along a gravel drive which narrows to a fenced path to a stone slab footbridge into a field. Go straight on across this field with more fine views of the Downs to your left to cross a footbridge and stile in its far right-hand corner. Now bear slightly left across the next field to join a grassy track in the far corner then take this track beside a right-hand hedge straight on. In the second field, where the track becomes fenced, cross a stile in the left-hand fence and follow the other side of the fence. Where the fence bears right, leave it and go straight on across the field to a gate and stile in the far hedge leading to a fenced track. Now turn immediately left off the track over a stile and footbridge and take path

CO7 through a belt of trees to a stile then continue across a field to cross two stiles in the next hedge just right of Ashen Copse Farm. Here bear half left across the next field to cross a stile just right of the farm then turn left along a grassy track passing right of the farm buildings to join a concrete track leading to a macadam farm road, part of the D'Arcy Dalton Way.

Cross this farm road and take path CO6 straight on over a stile by a gate and along a stony track bearing left to join the edge of Ashen Copse. At the far end of the copse take the track straight on along the edge of Flamborough Wood with more fine views of the Downs to your left. By the far end of Flamborough Wood turn right off the track and follow the edge of the wood for 50 yards then bear slightly left across former parkland to pass the right-hand edge of a clump of tall oaks. Here bear slightly left, with views across the Cole valley towards the Wiltshire town of Highworth on its hilltop to your left and towards Coleshill ahead, to cross a stile by the left-hand in a line of three oak trees at the bottom of the hill. Now pass right of an oak tree heading just right of a farm building with a white turret at Coleshill to cross stiles and a footbridge by a gated culvert then keep straight on across two further fields to a white gate right of a large stone house at Coleshill. Here take a macadam drive straight on ignoring a crossing drive and continuing to the B4019 opposite the village green with the remains of an ancient stone cross and the much restored Norman church with a fifteenth-century tower.

Until 1952 the hillside village of Coleshill, named after the nearby River Cole which forms the Wiltshire boundary, was an estate village ranged around a manor house built for Sir George Pratt between 1650 and 1662 to a design by the renowned architect Inigo Jones and said to be one of the latter's finest works. However in 1952 the house, which had later passed to the Pleydell-Bouverie family one of whom was made Earl of Radnor in 1765, was destroyed by fire and its ruins were demolished so that today all that remains are the gateposts, stables and a dovecote, while the park which you have just crossed is farmed by the National Trust.

Cross the B4019 and take Church Lane straight on past the church tower. At the far end of the lane go straight on through gates then turn right onto path CO1 beside a right-hand fence and hedge with wide views to your left across the Thames Valley towards the Cotswolds. Where the hedge turns right, bear slightly right across the field to a stile leading to a road junction. Cross the priority road and take path CO3 straight on through a hedge gap then follow a left-hand hedge straight on through two fields with fine views through the hedge across the Thames Valley towards the Cotswolds and soon ahead towards Badbury Hill and Forest. At the far side of the second field go straight on into Fern Copse. After 100 yards ignore a wide track to your right and keep straight on over a footbridge then a stile into a field. Now follow a left-hand hedge straight on to a stile then continue along a fenced path to a stile and footbridge. Here go straight on across a field corner to cross a footbridge and stile in the left-hand hedge some 10 yards beyond an electricity pole then bear half right across a field heading just left of the farmhouse at Brimstone Farm to cross a stile onto a farm track. Turn right onto this track crossing a concrete road and continuing through gates to a second concrete road.

Here take path CO4 straight on through more gates and follow the left-hand edge of a field to cross a gated culvert. Now take path GC4 beside a left-hand hedge to a field corner then turning right and following a left-hand hedge gently uphill to the edge of Coxwell Wood. Here take a defined path straight on uphill through the wood for a quarter mile ignoring all crossing or branching paths or tracks. At the top of Badbury Hill the path flattens out and widens into a track near a left-hand gate then gradually bears left, soon with an Iron Age hill fort clearly visible in the trees to your left, to reach a gate and stile into the picnic area.

WALK 22: BUSCOT

Length of Walk: (A) 10.5 miles / 17.0 Km
(B) 4.4 miles / 7.1 Km
Starting Point: Entrance to Buscot Weir National Trust Car Park.
Grid Ref: SU231977
Maps: OS Landranger Sheet 163
OS Explorer Sheet 170
OS Pathfinder Sheet 1135 (SU29/39)
How to get there / Parking: Buscot, 4 miles northwest of Faringdon, may be reached from the town by taking the A417 towards Lechlade. On entering Buscot village, turn right into the cul-de-sac village street where the National Trust Buscot Weir car park is on your right.
Notes: These walks should not be attempted when the River Thames is in flood. Walkers are also advised that the section of Walk A through Badbury Forest uses a permitted path which may be closed at any time and parts of which are badly drained. Should this path be closed or passage be difficult, a longer alternative route using definitive rights of way is shown on the plan.

Much of the village and parish of Buscot, bordering Gloucestershire and Wiltshire and formerly the most northwesterly village in Berkshire, is now owned and protected by the National Trust. Its riverside church, a third of a mile from the picturesque village centre, dates from about 1200 and is notable for its pulpit with panels believed to have been painted by the early sixteenth-century Flemish artist Jan Gossaert, known as Mabuse, and its east window by the pre-Raphaelite artist Sir Edward Burne-Jones. Paintings by Burne-Jones are also to be found in Buscot Park, an eighteenth-century stately home a mile southeast of the village which can be seen in the distance from both walks and whose parkland is skirted by Walk A. Burne-Jone's association with Buscot resulted from his visits to his friend and partner William Morris who bought a country retreat in the nearby 'earthly paradise' of Kelmscott in 1871.

Both walks lead you from the former Berkshire village of Buscot across the River Thames into Gloucestershire with glimpses of the fine fifteenth-century 'wool church' of Lechlade before entering 'old' Oxfordshire and visiting WIlliam Morris's Kelmscott. At Eaton Weir Walk A then recrosses the river skirting Buscot Park, exploring Badbury Forest and proceeding with fine views by way of the scattered village of Eaton Hastings back to Eaton Weir before both walks return along a pleasant stretch of Thames towpath to Buscot.

Both walks start from the entrance to Buscot Weir National Trust car park and turn right into the village street. At the end of the public road go through a squeeze-stile beside a gate and take path BS3 straight on along a private road. Where the road forks by a gate, bear right onto path BS11, a concrete road. Having crossed a bridge, turn right onto an enclosed path signposted to Lock Cottage passing the cottage and continuing to a bridge over Buscot Weir at the Gloucestershire boundary. At the far end of the bridge turn left onto fenced path LL28 soon crossing the lock gate at the left-hand end of Buscot Lock. Now, briefly joining the Thames Path, bear slightly left on paths LL27/28 to cross a bridge over a new weir then, leaving the Thames Path again, take path LL28 straight on over a stile into a field. Here bear half left heading left of Lechlade church spire crossing two small ditches to reach a culvert over a large fenced ditch. Now bear slightly left across the next field to a V-stile leading to two footbridges over watercourses constructed to regulate the flow of the Thames. At the far end of the second footbridge turn right soon crossing a V-stile onto a fenced farm track. Turn left onto this and follow it for half a mile ignoring a branching track to your right by Leaze Farm Dairy Unit and continuing to the Clanfield road.

Turn right onto this road and follow it for a third of a mile disregarding the first branching 'path' to your right and passing Paradise Farm. Just past the farm turn right over a stile by blue gates onto path LL21 bearing half left across a field to a gate in the far left-hand corner. Go through this and bear slightly left following a left-hand hedge through two fields. In the second field where the hedge turns left, bear slightly right across it to cross a footbridge and stiles at the Oxfordshire boundary. Now take path KM2 straight on across a large field towards a stone cottage at Kelmscott to reach a hedge gap onto a bend in the village road. Take this road straight on into this picturesque village with numerous fine stone-built houses and farm buildings with slate roofs eventually passing the church.

Originally built in the twelfth century, Kelmscott church is a small cruciform building with a bell gable from around 1300 and thirteenth-century murals and is notable for being virtually unaltered since the sixteenth century. Buried in the churchyard is William Morris, the pre-Raphaelite designer, interior decorator, writer and printer who bought the Elizabethan manor house in 1871 as a summer retreat and entertained his friends and partners there. After his death in 1896 his widow had Philip Webb design some cottages for the village and in 1934 the Morris Memorial Hall was built by Ernest Gimson and opened by the playwright, George Bernard Shaw.

Just past the church turn right onto the road signposted to Kelmscott Manor passing the Memorial Hall then by the Plough Inn and the base of an ancient cross turn right onto path KM1 passing through the pub car park. Now continue along a green lane which bears right by some gates. At the end of the lane turn left and follow a left-hand hedge. At the far side of the field go straight on over two footbridges then bear slightly right and follow a right-hand fence to cross a stile on the Thames Path (KM3).

On reaching the footbridge over the Thames at Eaton Weir, **Walk B** forks right continuing along the towpath. Now read the last paragraph. **Walk A** forks left onto path EH1 over the bridge into a car park. Bear slightly right across the car park to cross a stile by a gate then take a rough macadam road for nearly a mile with views of Buscot Park house in the trees ahead, ignoring branching roads to Kilmester Farm and continuing to the A417 opposite Buscot Park Lake.

Cross the main road, turn left onto its rough footway and follow it for a quarter mile to an old lodge. Just past the lodge turn right between ornamental gateposts onto bridleway EH7 (joining the D'Arcy Dalton Way) and follow a macadam farm road over a bridge at the end of the lake then continuing as bridleway BS13 for half a mile passing a small Greek temple and a cricket field with a thatched pavilion to your right to reach Oldfield Farm. Here, leaving the D'Arcy Dalton Way, turn left onto the farm road to Rowleaze Cottages where the road becomes bridleway EH8, then GC1 and then ends. Now go straight on through gates and follow a right-hand stream to pass through further gates then turn left onto path GC2 beside a left-hand hedge then the edge of

Rowleaze Wood. On reaching a fenced woodland clearing to your left, bear slightly right across the field to cross a footbridge and stile at the right-hand end of an outcrop of Oak Wood. Now follow the outside edge of the wood to cross stiles and a footbridge then bear slightly right across the next field to the corner of another outcrop of Oak Wood.

Here turn left through a bridlegate onto a waymarked permitted path through the wood. (If it is closed or passage is difficult, use the alternative route on the plan via paths GC2/GF23, bridleway GF3 and the A417.) On reaching a wide clearing, take a track right of a wooden shed straight on. Just before a gate into a field, fork left onto a branching track then just past a corner of the field turn right onto a track still following the inside edge of the wood. At a four-way junction go straight on then at a five-way junction (now in Eaton Wood) bear half right and follow a wide track for 300 yards to a junction of gravel roads. Here turn sharp left onto one of them then at the top of a slight rise turn sharp right onto a grassy track downhill through the woods ignoring two crossing tracks and continuing to a gate onto the A417.

Bear half right across this road and take path EH9, the rough road to Crabbe Tree Farm, which leads you over a hill with views of Faringdon to your right at first, then later ahead across the Thames valley towards the Cotswolds. At the farm go straight on past an electricity pole and through a gate then bear slightly left across the farmyard to cross a bridge left of a long shed into a field. Here turn right to cross a footbridge and stile then turn left gradually diverging from the left-hand fence to cross a stile and footbridge in the middle of the next hedge. Now bear slightly left up a field to cross a footbridge and stile right of two oak trees on the skyline then bear slightly left down the next field towards the farmhouse at Lower House Farm to reach gates on bridleway EH6. Go through these and bear left onto a farm road. At a T-junction with the public road to Eaton Hastings Church turn right onto it (briefly rejoining the D'Arcy Dalton Way).

On nearing the Norman church, at a sharp bend by the gates to Ferry Cottage, turn left over a stile by a gate onto path EH3 leaving the D'Arcy Dalton Way again and bear slightly left across a field passing just left of the left-hand corner of a cottage garden to cross a footbridge, stiles and the cottage drive. Now bear slightly right across the next field to cross another footbridge and stiles then keep straight on across two more fields crossing a footbridge and stile left of a cottage (where you ignore a stile to your right into the cottage garden) and continuing to a further stile. Cross this and bear slightly right to join the bank of a Thames backwater which you follow through three fields with views of Kelmscott in the trees to your right to reach a stile into the car park at Eaton Weir. Go straight on across this to a bridge on path EH1 then retrace your outward route past the cottage and over the Thames bridge. At the far end of the bridge turn left onto the Thames Path (KM3) rejoining Walk B.

Walks A and B now follow the Thames towpath (KM3, later LL27) for 1.3 miles, soon with views of Buscot Park house in trees a mile away to your left and later passing two of the wartime 'pill-boxes' or anti-aircraft gun emplacements to be found all along the Thames which enemy aircraft followed for navigation purposes. On nearing Buscot, turn left over a modern concrete bridge over the new weir stream and follow the left-hand edge of an island to Buscot Lock. At the far end of the lock, leaving the Thames Path, turn left over the lock gates and retrace your steps along paths LL28, BS11 and BS3 into Buscot.

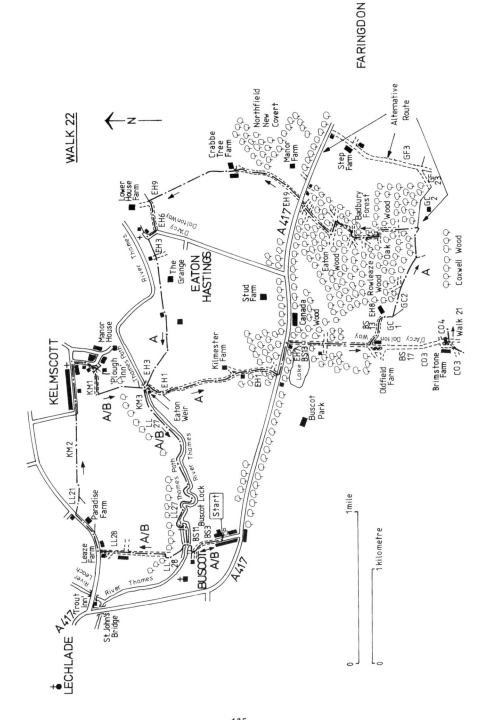

WALK 22

135

Length of Walk: (A) 9.8 miles / 15.8 Km
                      (B) 1.7 miles / 2.8 Km
                      (C) 8.3 miles / 13.3 Km
Starting Point: (A/B) Faringdon Market Place.
                      (C)   'Anchor Inn', Church Green,
                             Stanford-in-the-Vale.
Grid Ref: (A/B) SU289956 / (C) SU343935
Maps: OS Landranger Sheets 163 (A&B only) & 164 (all)
             OS Explorer Sheet 170
             OS Pathfinder Sheet 1135 (SU29/39)
How to get there / Parking: (A/B) Walkers on Walk B can use the signposted (short-stay) car park in Southampton Street, Faringdon. For Walk A take London Street towards Faringdon Folly then turn right into Stanford Road, where unrestricted on-street parking is available.
(C) See Walk 24.

Faringdon today is a quiet country town with a fine seventeenth-century Town Hall and a number of picturesque inns, houses and shops from the same period. The uniform age of many of these buildings is an indication of the town's less peaceful past, as in 1645–6 Faringdon was besieged by Parliamentary forces who destroyed the church spire together with much of the town. The cruciform church, which otherwise survived the bombardment, dates largely from the twelfth and thirteenth centuries and contains monuments to the Unton and Pye families who dominated the town for several hundred years. Faringdon House to the north of the church was built by the undistinguished poet laureate Henry James Pye in 1780 but had to be sold later to pay off his debts, while its park is said to be haunted by the headless ghost of Hampden Pye who had his head blown off in a sea battle before a plot by his step-mother to have him murdered could come to fruition. In the 1930s this house was acquired by the reputedly eccentric musician, author and playwright, Lord Berners, who in 1935 had the Faringdon Folly erected on Faringdon Hill on the site of an Iron Age hill fort, a twelfth-century castle and the battery used by Cromwell to destroy the town. This 140 foot-high tower, erected to give work to the local unemployed with its fine views across the county and beyond, is thought to be the last major folly to be built in Britain.

Walks A and B lead you from Faringdon to this fine viewpoint and return by way of Church Path with more fine views, while Walks A and C explore the remote flat country scattered with woods in the Ock valley to the east visiting the fascinating small villages of Hatford and Shellingford as well as the larger village of Stanford-in-the-Vale (described in the introduction to Walk 24).

Walks A and B start from Faringdon Market Place and take London Street (signposted to Faringdon Folly) for 300 yards. Just past a pub called 'The Folly' turn right into Stanford Road and take its raised left-hand footway. By some white safety railings to your right turn left onto walled macadamed path GF13 climbing steadily. Near the top of Folly Hill, where the Folly comes into view ahead, at the edge of its surrounding copse turn right onto path GF15 following a left-hand fence round the hilltop first with views of Faringdon to your right and the Downs ahead and later with Didcot Power Station and the distant Chilterns coming into view ahead. On the far side of the hilltop turn right onto crossing path GF13 and follow it downhill keeping right of a hedge and going through a gap by a disused stile where **Walk B** turns left onto path LW1 beside a left-hand hedge. Now read the last paragraph.

Walks A and C now take path LW13 straight on downhill towards Wadley Manor with fine views across the Vale of the White Horse towards Didcot Power Station and the Chilterns ahead and the Downs to your right. At the bottom hedge cross a stile, the A420 Faringdon Bypass and a stile opposite and take a grassy track beside a right-hand hedge straight on. At the far end of the field cross a rail-stile by white gates then bear half right across a field heading towards Didcot Power Station to cross an old fenceline some 50 yards left of gates at a track junction. Now cross the track and go straight on across the next field to a gate and rails at the right-hand end of a belt of trees leading to a junction of grassy tracks.

Here take path HF6 bearing half right onto one of these tracks to reach the left-hand corner of Chinham Copse. Now bear slightly left and follow the outside edge of the copse then a right-hand hedge until the track turns right through a gate in the hedge. Here leave the track and follow the right-hand hedge straight on to a corner of the field where you go straight on through a copse. On re-emerging into the field, bear half right into an overgrown wood called Lower Tagdown Plantation and follow the winding ill-defined path for nearly half a mile crossing a footbridge at one point and continuing until you re-emerge over a sleeper footbridge into a field. Now follow Frogmore Brook to your right straight on along the edge of a tree belt for a third of a mile to the road to a gravel pit. Here go straight on over a stile by a gate and continue to follow the brook through two young plantations and four fields with Hatford coming into view ahead. In the fourth field near Manor House Farm turn right over a gated culvert then left onto path SV22 along the right bank of the brook to a stile onto the B4508 on the edge of Hatford.

This tiny village has a Norman church referred to in the Domesday Book which in 1555 was the scene of the wedding of Anne Seymour, daughter of the Duke of Somerset and Lord Protector to young Edward VI, to Sir Edward Unton of Wadley Hall. Due to its ruinous condition, it was closed in 1873 and replaced by a new church, but 100 years later the old church was restored and reopened and its Victorian replacement was declared redundant and sold.

Turn left onto the B4508 crossing a bridge over Frogmore Brook then turn right over a stile by a gate onto path HF9 bearing slightly left across a field heading left of a cottage to cross a stile onto its drive. Here turn right along the drive. At a fork by the cottage take a green lane straight on to a gate and stile into a field. Now bear half left passing just left of an electricity pole and continuing to the far corner of the field. Here step over a low barbed-wire fence, turn right over a footbridge and take enclosed path SV3 straight on for a quarter mile, eventually widening into a lane and reaching a green at Stanford-in-the-Vale. Do **NOT** join the road but turn right onto macadam path SV19 along the back of the green then continue across the green to join a macadam drive then Cottage Road. Just past Cottage Farm turn left between safety barriers onto path SV5 and follow it straight on past the end of an estate road to a bend in Joyce's Road. Turn right onto this road then immediately left onto path SV6. On entering the churchyard, **Walk C** turns left onto path SV20 to return to your starting point while **Walk A** takes path SV6 straight on.

Walk C starts from the 'Anchor Inn' at Church Green, Stanford-in-the-Vale crossing the road and taking a side road towards the church then takes path SV20 straight on through the churchyard passing right of the church. On reaching crossing path SV6, turn left onto it. **Walks A and C (and Walk 24)** now take path SV6 leaving the churchyard and keeping straight on to the end of a cul-de-sac road. Follow this to a T-junction then take fenced path SV23 straight on to reach High Street. Turn right onto this **(leaving Walk 24)** and follow it to the A417 onto which you turn right. Just past the 'Horse and Jockey' turn left onto path SV4 along a macadam, then gravel drive. By some ornamental gateposts fork right off the drive onto a fenced grassy path leading to a stile. Here cross a track and bear slightly left across a field with a fine view of White Horse Hill to your left to cross rails by a gate then follow a left-hand fence straight on. Near the far end of the field bear slightly right across its corner to a stile, footbridge and stone stile then bear slightly right across the next field to a footbridge in the next hedge. Here bear slightly right across another field to cross a footbridge and stile in the far corner. Now take path SF6 bearing slightly right across a field to two stiles flanking a farm track some 60 yards right of a copse. Cross these and bear half right across two fields to a hunting-gate at the left-hand end of Fishpond Copse where you cross a bridge and enter the copse.

After 10 yards turn left through another hunting-gate into a field then turn right passing under a willow tree to reach a gate left of a barn where Shellingford comes into view ahead. Here bear slightly right across a field to a stile then turn right onto path SF4 along a fenced concrete track to gates into a farmyard. Just past a silage clamp turn left through gates onto a concrete track soon bearing right then forking left to a handgate into Church Street opposite the Norman church with its thirteenth-century tower and seventeenth-century steeple rebuilt in 1852 after it was struck by lightning. The village, originally called Sevenge Ford and later Shellingford Newbury, was once the site of an annual fair suppressed by force in 1276 by Fulk Fitz Warin of Wantage to eliminate competition with Wantage Fair.

Turn left into Church Street. After 120 yards, opposite a white gate, turn left over a stile onto path SF7 crossing a field to a 'stile' in its far right-hand corner. Now bear left between hedges to another stile then keep straight on across a field, with fine views to your left towards White Horse Hill, to cross a stile by two tall conifers onto the B4508. Turn right onto this road then immediately left onto path SF5 along a short green lane to a gate into a field. Bear slightly left across this large field, soon with more fine views of the Downs to your left and a view of Kitemore House to your right, heading right of Wicklesham Lodge Farm on a hilltop ahead and a large chestnut tree at the far side of the field, to reach a footbridge and kissing-gate by an oak tree in the far corner of the field. Now go straight on passing right of a chestnut tree to reach a hedge gap between a chestnut tree and a tall elm. Here bear slightly left heading for an oak tree left of Wickwood Farm (the nearer of two farms ahead) to cross a fence in the field corner. (NB If there is no stile here, use the gate in the right-hand hedge.) Now bear half right across the next field towards the left side of the farm buildings at Wickwood Farm.

At the farm turn right onto the remnants of a concrete track to reach a gate onto a concrete drive. Follow this straight on to a T-junction, then turn left through a gate and immediately right through a hunting-gate, passing a bungalow to your left and crossing a sheep-wire fence. Now bear slightly left across a field to a sleeper footbridge in the middle of a row of four tall elms some 30 yards left of the bottom corner of the field. Continue through the tree belt to a second footbridge then take path GF19 straight on out of the trees. Now turn right over a culvert, then bear left across a field towards a midfield tree in front of Wicklesham Lodge Farm on its hilltop. Halfway across the field, turn right onto crossing bridleway GF20 heading for a clump of bushes left of a midfield oak and near the end of a thick hedge. Pass left of these bushes to reach a track junction, then take a farm track straight on beside a right-hand fence. Where the fence bears right, follow the track bearing slightly left down the field to a track junction and hedge gap in the valley bottom. Here take bridleway GF21 straight on over a culvert then follow a farm track beside a left-hand hedge. Where the hedge bears left, leave it and take the track uphill towards a house gradually bearing right to join a right-hand fence and continuing to the A417 onto which you turn left. At a T-junction cross the A420 Faringdon Bypass and turn right onto its far verge looking out for a signpost to your left where you take path LW1. Do **NOT** enter a field **BUT** turn right and take a path between a left-hand hedge and a right-hand plantation to pass through a gap by a redundant stile. Now follow a left-hand hedge up the side of Folly Hill until you reach a stile and gap in the hedge where **Walk A** follows the hedge straight on while **Walk C** turns right onto path LW13. (Now go back eight paragraphs.)

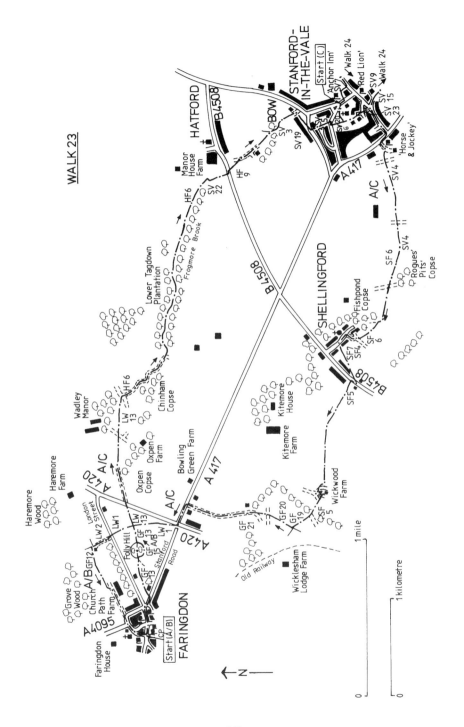

WALK 23

STANFORD-IN-THE-VALE

Start (C)
'Anchor Inn'
Walk 24
'Red Lion'
Walk 24
SV7
SV9
SV 15
SV 23
HATFORD
B4508
BOW
SV 3
SV19
SV6
'Horse & Jockey'
A417
A/C
SV4
Manor House Farm
HF 9
HF6
SV 22
Lower Tagdown Plantation
Frogmore Brook
SHELLINGFORD
Fishpond Copse
SF7
SF6
SF6
SF4
SV4
Rogues' Pits' Copse
SF 5
Wadley Manor
HF6
LW 13
Chinham Copse
B4508
Kitemore House
Kitemore Farm
SF5
B4508
Haremore Wood
Haremore Farm
A/C
A420
Oxpen Copse
Oxpen Farm
Bowling Green Farm
A417
Wickwood Farm
London Street
LW1
LW2
LW 13
GF 13
LW
GF 13
LW 1
A/C
A420
Stanford Road
GF20
GF 19
GF 21
SF 5
Wickklesham Lodge Farm
Old Railway
Grove Wood
Church A/B
GF12
Folly Hill
GF 13
GF 13
A/B
Faringdon House
A4095
CP
Start (A/B)
FARINGDON

1 mile

1 kilometre

0

0

←N—

141

Walks A and B now take path LW1 straight on beside a left-hand hedge to a stile onto London Street. Bear slightly left across it to go through a gap by a gate onto path LW2 which follows the fenced drive to Grove Lodge downhill with fine views across the Thames Valley towards the Cotswolds. By the house leave the drive and go straight on to a waymarked crossways by the bottom corner of its garden. Here turn left onto fenced path GF12 known as Church Path. Follow this for a third of a mile, with more fine views to your right, to reach two squeeze stiles onto a farm road by Church Path Farm. Continue along this road to a bend in a public road then take Church Street straight on, joining the A4095 and passing some Victorian farm cottages and the church to reach the Market Place.

WALK 24: STANFORD-IN-THE-VALE

Length of Walk: 7.9 miles / 12.7 Km
Starting Point: 'Anchor Inn', Church Green,
Stanford-in-the-Vale.
Grid Ref: SU343935
Maps: OS Landranger Sheets 164 or 174
OS Explorer Sheet 170
OS Pathfinder Sheet 1135 (SU29/39)
How to get there / Parking: Stanford-in-the-Vale, 3.5 miles
southeast of Faringdon, may be reached from the town by
taking the A417 towards Wantage. On reaching Stanford-
in-the-Vale, take the second turning left into the village and
follow it to Church Green then look for a suitable place to
park.

Stanford-in-the-Vale, in the midst of the Ock valley better known as the Vale of the White Horse, is a large scattered village with several greens and many picturesque cottages, some of which are thatched. Judging from the size of the village, its greens and its parish church, Stanford-in-the-Vale would appear to have once been a place of some importance and indeed from 1250 onwards it was a market town famous for cheese-making, but the market later declined and ceased, as did the cheese-making. The large late twelfth-century church has an ancient pulpit and a carved wooden font and cover while its bells were acquired in 1970 from St. Peter-in-the-East, Oxford when this disused church was converted into St. Edmund Hall's college library.

The walk explores the quiet, flat country to the east of Stanford-in-the-Vale visiting the fascinating rural villages of Goosey with its enormous green and Denchworth and Charney Bassett with their ancient manor houses. Despite being easy in nature and varying in height by less than 50 feet throughout the walk, the countryside is by no means monotonous with numerous views from slight rises in the ground, particularly of the Downs.

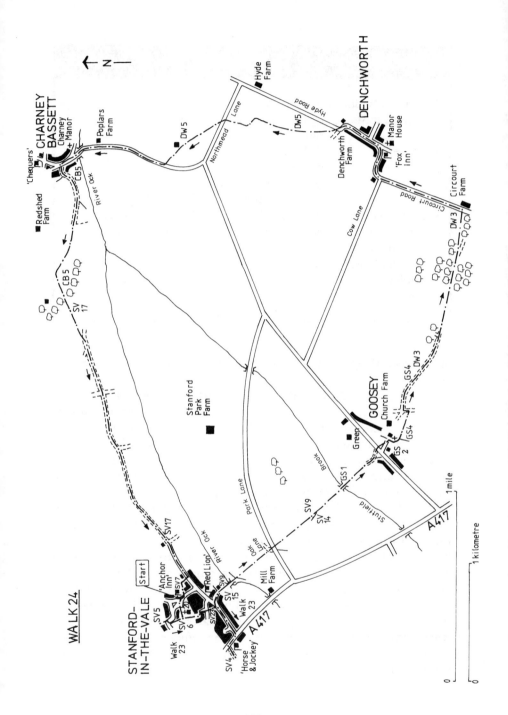

WALK 24

← N —

STANFORD-IN-THE-VALE

CHARNEY BASSETT

DENCHWORTH

GOOSEY

1 mile

1 kilometre

Starting from the 'Anchor Inn' at Church Green, Stanford-in-the-Vale, cross the road and take a side road towards the church then take path SV20 straight on through the churchyard passing right of the church. On reaching a crossing path (SV6), turn left onto it (**joining Walk 23**) leaving the churchyard and keeping straight on to reach the end of a cul-de-sac road. Follow this to a T-junction then take fenced path SV23 straight on to reach High Street. Turn left onto this (**leaving Walk 23**) then immediately right into Marlborough Lane (SV15) bearing right by a stone-built shed. By a modern house bear slightly right onto path SV9 along a grassy gravel drive. Where this bears left, leave it and take a fenced path straight on to a footbridge over the River Ock and a stile into a field. Here follow the Ock straight on at first then bear slightly right across the field with views of the Downs to your right, passing through gates in the right-hand fence and continuing to a gate and stile left of the far right-hand corner of the field. Cross the stile then take a green lane called Oak Lane straight on to gates into Park Lane.

Cross this road and the left-hand of two footbridges opposite and take path SV9 beside a right-hand hedge around two sides of a field to a footbridge and stile. Here go straight on across two fields to a stile and footbridge at the far right-hand corner of the second field. Now bear slightly right across the next field to cross a footbridge in a bend in Stutfield Brook near the left-hand end of a row of willows then take path GS1 bearing slightly right and passing a redundant stile and the right-hand end of a hedge to reach concealed gates in the far corner of the field leading to a stony track. Take this track straight on to Goosey Green reaching the road by a postbox. As its name suggests, this green was once used for the rearing of geese and the village, though small, is one of great age as it was given to Abingdon Abbey in the eighth century by King Offa of Mercia (after whom Offa's Dyke is named) in exchange for Andersey Island.

Bear slightly right across the green to its far right-hand corner by the church then turn right onto path GS2 through gates into the churchyard. Here fork right off the path to the church, passing right of this tiny thirteenth-century church with a bellcot then bearing left to a stile in the rear left-hand corner of the churchyard. Cross this, a footbridge and another stile and take path GS4 beside a left-hand hedge, wiggling right at one point then going straight on across the field to its far left-hand corner. Here turn left through a gate then right through a second and take a stony track across the field to a gap in the far hedge. Now take path DW3 straight on along its grassy continuation through two fields. At the far side of the second field ignore a fork to your left and go straight on through a gate and across a third field to a gate left of a clump of willows concealing a pond. Now take a grassy track straight on through a plantation to a gap in its top hedge. Go through this, then turn left into a field. Now bear right across the field to a stile onto Circourt Road opposite the right-hand end of the red-brick farmhouse at Circourt Farm. Turn left onto this road and follow it for two-thirds of a mile ignoring Cow Lane to your left and entering Denchworth.

Like Goosey, Denchworth was also in the hands of Abingdon Abbey in mediaeval times. Following the Dissolution their moated manor house was largely rebuilt by William Hyde and was visited by Amy Robsart, wife of royal favourite Lord Robert Dudley, prior to her mysterious death at Cumnor in 1560. It is this house, through somewhat extended, which has survived till the present day. In the much-altered Norman church, once famed for its collection of chained books which included a Cranmer bible dated 1541 and 'Golden Legend' in an original Caxton printing from 1483 (now in the Bodleian Library in Oxford), is, amongst others, a brass depicting William Hyde and his large family which was found during restoration of the church by the renowned Victorian architect, George Street of Wantage to have been reused as the reverse side bears an inscription in Norman French from which it transpires that the brass must have originated in Bisham Abbey (near Marlow) in or after 1333.

By the 'Fox Inn' turn left. At another junction with an ancient market cross, take the West Hanney, Charney Bassett and Longworth road straight on. At the far end of the village at a sharp right-hand bend leave the road and take path DW5 straight on through the right-hand of three gates into a field then bear half right across it, with wide views to your left towards Folly Hill near Faringdon and over your left shoulder towards the Downs, to reach a stile. Now bear slightly left across the next field to a gap in its far hedge then go straight on across a third field to a stile and footbridge left of a small oak tree in the far hedge. Here bear half left across the corner of the next field to cross a stile by a gate then turn right beside a right-hand hedge to a gate into Northmead Lane. Cross this road and a stile by a gate opposite then (still on path DW5) bear half left across a field to cross a footbridge and stile in the middle of the left-hand hedge. Here go straight on across the next field to cross a stile and footbridge under an oak tree then bear slightly right to cross two stiles. Now follow a left-hand fence, then a line of young poplars, to a footbridge onto a road. Turn right onto this and follow it for half a mile to a bridge over the River Ock into Charney Bassett.

To your right are the tiny village church, which is of Norman origin but largely rebuilt in the fifteenth century and given its bellcot 200 years later, and Charney Manor with its mullioned windows. Now owned by the Society of Friends, Charney Manor was built by Abingdon Abbey between 1250 and 1280 as a grange of Abingdon Abbey and as such is one of the oldest surviving mediaeval manor houses.

Now take Main Street straight on then by a telephone box turn left into Bridle Path (CB5). Where this gravel lane ends, bear half left into a narrow green lane and follow it for a third of a mile, briefly entering a field and later ignoring a branching path to your left. On reaching a bridlegate, go straight on through this and follow a left-hand hedge soon passing through a further gate into a fenced bridleway. Continue along this, briefly with an enclosing right-hand hedge, until you reach a bridlegate where a second gate to your right leads to a private drive. Here turn left onto a grassy track, passing through a further gate and following a left-hand fence and sporadic hedge straight on to a gate and stone bridge into a green lane, soon crossing a further gated stone bridge to enter a field. Here take bridleway SV17 bearing half right across the field towards Stanford-in-the-Vale Church to reach a gate in the far hedge right of two ash trees. Go through this and follow a grassy track beside a left-hand fence through two fields to reach a crossing track. Now take the track straight on for nearly another mile to reach the end of a macadam road at Stanford-in-the-Vale. Take this road straight on for 350 yards into the village then, where a left-hand pavement begins, turn right onto enclosed path SV7 soon bearing left and emerging at the side of the 'Anchor Inn'.

Length of Walk: 5.1 miles / 8.3 Km
Starting Point: Entrance to Longworth Church.
Grid Ref: SU385994
Maps: OS Landranger Sheet 164
OS Explorer Sheets 170 & 180
OS Pathfinder Sheets 1115 (SP20/30) &
1135 (SU29/39)

How to get there / Parking: Longworth, 7 miles west of
Abingdon, may be reached from the town by taking the A415
towards Witney for 6.8 miles crossing the A338 and A420.
Having crossed the A420, take the first turning left towards
Longworth and Hinton Waldrist. On reaching Longworth,
turn right into Cow Lane into the village. At the far end of the
village street turn right into Church Lane and follow it to its
end by the church and Longworth Manor where parking is
possible.

Notes: This walk should not be attempted when the River
Thames is in flood as parts of it are prone to flooding.

Longworth on the low ridge separating the valleys of the Thames
and the Ock (better known as the Vale of the White Horse) was
once noted as a centre of rose-growing when the local firm Messrs.
Tucker & Drew was in its prime and even today the village's
gardens bear witness to this. Though off the beaten track even
before the ancient Oxford–Bristol road was rerouted away from
Appleton Road to run through Kingston Bagpuize, Longworth is
not without historical significance as in the seventeenth century
Longworth Manor was home to Sir Henry Marten who signed
Charles I's death warrant. At the Restoration this led to his
imprisonment by Charles II in Chepstow Castle and it was only by
forfeiting Longworth to Charles's chief minister, Edward Hyde,
that Marten escaped execution. Also in the same century
Longworth was the birthplace of Dr John Fell, the author and
architect who designed Tom Tower at Christ Church College,

Oxford and was responsible for the transfer to it from the cathedral of the mighty bell known as Great Tom, while two hundred years later the village saw the birth of R D Blackmore, author of 'Lorna Doone'. The twelfth-century church, which was extended in the next century and has a fifteenth-century tower, also contains a brass commemorating Dr Illingworth, a celebrated rector who hosted annual meetings of church leaders at the Old Rectory during his incumbency from 1883 to 1915 and from one of these meetings in 1889 resulted a celebrated theological work known as 'Lux Mundi'.

The walk leads you from Longworth with its fine views northwards across the Thames Valley by way of another vantage point at Harrowdown Hill to a particularly remote section of the Thames towpath then follows this upstream past the fascinating deserted village of Shifford to the picturesque ford at Duxford on the ancient course of the river. You then proceed by way of Duxford hamlet and uphill to the ridgetop village of Hinton Waldrist before skirting Longworth Manor on the way back to your starting point.

Starting by the entrance to Longworth Church take Church Lane back towards the village. At a right-hand bend leave the road and take path LH3 straight on through a gate left of a cottage following a right-hand hedge through the village allotments. At the far side of the allotments turn left still following a right-hand hedge and soon bearing right with fine views ahead across the Thames Valley towards Harrowdown Hill immediately ahead and Wytham Hill and Cumnor Hurst to your right. On reaching a kissing-gate, go through it and turn right along a fenced track. Where the track turns right, go straight on through two kissing-gates into Tuck's Lane. Turn left onto this road and follow it downhill bearing left and left again to its end by the entrance to a cottage called 'Tucksmead'.

Here turn right onto path LH1 and take this green lane over Harrowdown Hill with fine views to your right towards Wytham Hill, Cumnor Hurst and Boars Hill. On emerging between wooden posts into a field, ignore a crossing track and follow a left-hand hedge straight on. At the far end of the field continue through bushes to cross a hump-backed stone bridge over the original course of the Thames (now dry) and a stile then keep straight on joining the towpath and Thames

Path (SK10) and following it to a kissing-gate in a line of willow trees where you recross the original course of the river. Now continue along the towpath (successively as LH16, AB9, LH17 and HW1) for over a mile passing the hamlet of Shifford on the opposite bank.

Shifford, which now comprises a tiny Victorian church, a farm and a few cottages, must in mediaeval times have been a place of some importance as in the ninth century King Alfred is said to have held an early English parliament there and in 1279 twenty-three households were recorded, but inclosure in the fifteenth century is thought to be the cause of its depopulation. Until the 1850s Shifford on a slight rise was frequently cut off by floods which inundated vast areas of the Bampton Polderland, but as a result of William Bryan Wood's ingenious drainage scheme which accompanied the enclosure of neighbouring Aston Bampton, this problem was considerably alleviated. The centrepiece of this scheme was the creation of Great Brook by straightening and improving the existing Isle of Wight Brook to accommodate the excess water and it is this waterway which flows into the Thames near Shifford Church.

Having passed Shifford, continue upstream on path HW1 for a further mile past the mouth of Shifford Lock Cut, constructed to enable river traffic to bypass the shallows at Duxford Ford and the newly-constructed footbridge which takes the Thames Path over the old river, later with scrub hiding the river from view in places. On descending a flight of steps to reach Duxford Ford, which despite its treacherous current was once an important crossing point of the upper Thames, fork left onto bridleway HW9 and follow its obvious course for 250 yards past two attractive thatched stone cottages to the road at Duxford. Turn left onto this road and follow it for three-quarters of a mile, eventually climbing through woodland to reach the hilltop village of Hinton Waldrist.

Hinton Waldrist with its stone cottages and high stone walls, like Longworth, is a village of some historical interest. Built on the site of a Roman earthwork called Achester which probably served to defend access to Duxford Ford, the village is also the site of a mediaeval castle of the Norman St. Valery family, of whose name Waldrist is thought to be a corruption. The earthworks of this castle are still visible in the grounds of the Elizabethan manor house which Charles I granted to Sir Henry Marten, only for his son to display ingratitude by signing the king's death warrant.

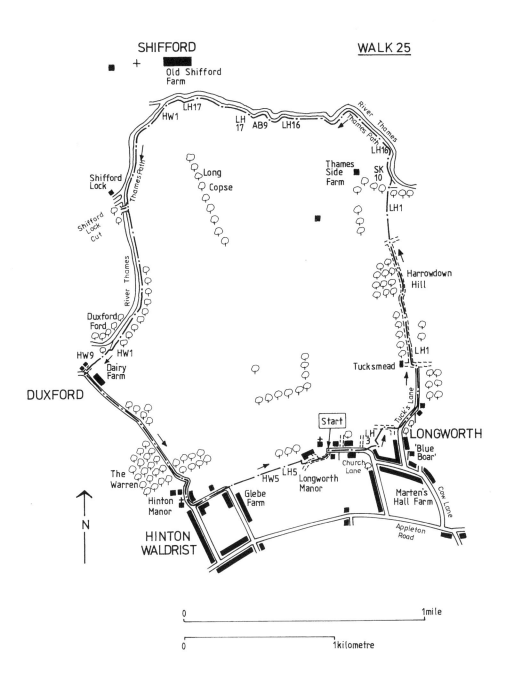

SHIFFORD

Old Shifford
Farm

LH17
HW1
LH
17 AB9 LH16

River Thames
Thames Path
LH16

Shifford
Lock

Thames Path

Long
Copse

Thames
Side
Farm

SK
10

LH1

Shifford
Lock
Cut

River Thames

Harrowdown
Hill

LH1

Duxford
Ford

Tucksmead

HW9 HW1

DUXFORD

Dairy
Farm

Tuck's Lane

Start

LONGWORTH

LH
3

'Blue
Boar'

The
Warren

HW5 LH5

Longworth
Manor

Church
Lane

Marten's
Hall Farm

Cow Lane

N

Hinton
Manor

Glebe
Farm

HINTON
WALDRIST

Appleton
Road

0   1mile

0   1kilometre

Just past the church, which is largely thirteenth-century but heavily restored, turn left at a road junction. At a right-hand bend leave the road and take fenced bridleway HW5 straight on with fine views through gaps in the left-hand hedge across the Thames Valley and the tops of the Downs just visible to your right. At the far end of the right-hand field where Longworth Church and outbuildings of the Manor come into view ahead, take fenced bridleway LH5 straight on, bearing right then left by the Manor outbuildings then ignoring a branching track to your right and joining a macadam drive. Take this straight on past Longworth Manor and an attractive pond to reach gates leading to your starting point.

Length of Walk: 9.1 miles / 14.6 Km
Starting Point: Entrance to the car park at the junction of Back Lane and Clover Place, Eynsham.
Grid Ref: SP431094
Maps: OS Landranger Sheet 164
OS Explorer Sheet 180
OS Pathfinder Sheets 1115 (SP20/30) & 1116 (SP40/50)
How to get there / Parking: Eynsham, 5.5 miles northwest of Oxford City Centre, may be reached from the Ring Road north of the City by taking the A40 towards Witney and Cheltenham to its junction with the B4449. Turn left onto the B4449 towards Stanton Harcourt and Standlake then turn immediately right onto a road into Eynsham. After nearly half a mile turn right into Spareacre Lane (signposted to a car park and toilets) then turn left into Back Lane and follow it for some 350 yards to a car park on the left at a right-angle bend.
Notes: Do not attempt this walk when the Thames is in flood.

Eynsham, pronounced 'Enshem', a small former market town with a picturesque centre which has grown considerably in recent years, is a place of great antiquity as there is evidence of neolithic inhabitation of the area and it is mentioned as 'Egonesham' in the Anglo-Saxon Chronicle of AD 571. In mediaeval times the town must have been of some importance as Aethelmar founded a Benedictine abbey here in 1005, whose first abbot was the renowned bible translator Aelfric, and in 1135 a market was established, from which the unusually tall market cross and the seventeenth-century Market House survive. By the market square is also the fourteenth-century church with a fifteenth-century tower and a fine mural of St. Catherine but the nearby abbey was demolished following its suppression in 1539. This seems to mark the beginning of Eynsham's decline as, despite its location on the ancient Gloucester turnpike road, the market ceased and by the

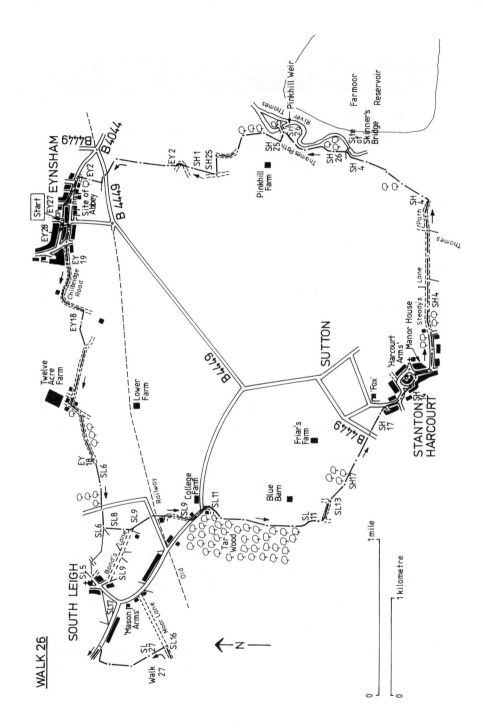

WALK 26

SOUTH LEIGH

EYNSHAM

Start

SUTTON

STANTON HARCOURT

1 mile

1 kilometre

←N—

1930s, when it was bypassed by the modern A40, it was little more than a sleepy country village.

The walk, which despite its length is easy in nature, explores the quiet low-lying country between the Windrush and the Thames, first leading you westwards from Eynsham across gently rising ground with wide views to the edge of the scattered village of South Leigh before turning south past Tar Wood to the picturesque village of Stanton Harcourt with its thatched stone cottages and fascinating mediaeval manor house. You then continue by way of Thames-side meadows eventually returning to Eynsham.

Starting from the entrance to the car park take Clover Place westwards. After some 50 yards turn left onto path EY28, an alleyway called Wastie Lane leading to Acre End Street, onto which you turn right. At a mini-roundabout take Chilbridge Road (bridleway EY19) straight on, soon leaving the village behind, crossing Chil Bridge and passing a farm. Having rounded a sharp left-hand bend there is a fine view of Wytham Hill to your left then at the top of a rise look out for a kissing-gate in the right-hand hedge. Turn right through this onto path EY18 going straight across a field to a stile between two electricity poles. Here bear slightly left across the next field to reach a bend in a farm road just before the near end of a hedge. Turn right onto this road and follow it gently uphill, with views to your right towards Eynsham Hall, a large Victorian mansion and to your left across the wide expanse of the Thames Valley towards the distant Downs, to reach Twelve Acre Farm.

At the farm, at a fork, go straight on between a barn and a green-painted concrete building to a junction of drives by the farmhouse. Here turn left onto a track beside a left-hand hedge. Where the track forks, bear right along a grassy track beside a right-hand hedge. At the far end of the hedge take the track straight on, dropping gently to a gap in the next hedge left of an oak tree. Here take path SL6 straight on, keeping right of a hedge to a stile and footbridge then go through a hedge gap and follow a right-hand hedge gently uphill to a stile onto the Barnard Gate road. Bear half left across this road and a footbridge and stile virtually opposite then follow a left-hand hedge to a corner of the field. Here go straight on through a hedge gap then turn left onto path SL8 following a left-hand hedge downhill. At the bottom corner of the field go through a concealed hedge gap some 20 yards right of the field corner into Bonds Lane (SL9) then turn left onto it almost immediately entering a field. Here continue across the field to a hedge gap and bridlebridge onto the Barnard Gate road just left of a row of cypress trees.

Cross the road and a bridlebridge opposite then follow the row of trees crossing the former Oxford–Witney railway line (opened in 1861 and closed in 1962) to join a macadam drive by some farm buildings. Take this drive straight on with fine views of Wytham Hill and Cumnor Hurst to your left. On reaching a public road, turn left onto it and follow it along the edge of Tar Wood. At the far side of the wood, fork right off the road onto path SL11, a gravel track past a concealed cottage. Where the track turns right through a gate to some garages, leave it and follow the outside edge of Tar Wood straight on for two-thirds of a mile through two fields. At the far end of the wood follow a right-hand hedge straight on to reach a bend in a gravel track then turn left onto this track now on path SL13. Where the track turns left towards the inappropriately-named Blue Barn, leave it and bear half right across a field to a corner of a hedge. Here turn left over a culvert in a hedge gap then turn right onto path SH17 following a right-hand hedge for a third of a mile to a stile onto the B4449. Cross this road and a stile opposite and follow a right-hand hedge straight on to a hedge gap leading to a village street in Stanton Harcourt.

Turn right onto this road ignoring a turning signposted to Hardwick and Witney then at a left-hand bend by Leena Cottage turn right onto hedged concrete path SH14 leading to a residential cul-de-sac, onto which you turn right. At its far end take path SH14 left of a row of council houses straight on, gradually bearing left past a thatched cottage to reach a road opposite the Manor House which is sometimes open to the public. Stanton Harcourt Manor has been held by the Harcourt family since the twelfth century and part of the present house including the Great Kitchen dates from about 1380. This enormous kitchen is thought now to be unique as it has no chimneys but adjustable louvres in its fifteenth-century roof which could be opened or closed according to the wind direction to allow the smoke to escape. Much of the old house was demolished in the eighteenth century when the Harcourts built a new house in Cokethorpe Park, but among the other surviving parts is Pope's Tower dating from 1470 which is so called as the poet Alexander Pope stayed there in 1718 while working on his translation of Homer's 'Iliad'. In 1948, following the sale of a later house at Nuneham

Courtenay, the Harcourts reoccupied Stanton Harcourt Manor and extended the house and remodelled its garden into their present form.

Turn right onto this road passing some attractive thatched cottages then after 180 yards turn left into Steady's Lane with fine views to your left of the Manor House complex and the church dating from about 1150 but later enlarged. After a quarter mile where the macadam road forks, take bridleway (then footpath) SH4 straight on along a private road for nearly a mile, later joining the Thames Path and with views of Wytham Hill to your left. Where the road ends at a gate and kissing-gate, go through the kissing-gate and turn left following a left-hand hedge to a gate. Now continue diagonally across the next meadow to a gated farm bridge then bear left over a culvert to a further gate. Here go straight on crossing a meadow diagonally to join the bank of the River Thames where a low grass bank on the other side of the river conceals the vast Farmoor Reservoir. Now follow the riverbank until a barbed-wire fence prevents your way forward. Until the 1940s the river was crossed at this point by a footbridge known as Skinner's Bridge, the concrete foundations of which can be seen on the opposite bank, but this was unfortunately destroyed by fire and the Oxford Fieldpaths Society is currently seeking it reconstruction.

Here turn left onto path SH26 following a fence beside a backwater covered in summer with numerous waterlilies. After the fence ends, continue along the riverbank eventually rejoining the main stream. Now cross two stiles and a footbridge and follow the riverbank to a kissing-gate, then bear slightly right, leaving the river and aiming for Pinkhill Weir. On reaching a kissing-gate leading to the weir, DO NOT go through it, but, leaving the Thames Path, turn sharp left onto path SH25 heading for a red iron gate. DO NOT go through this either, but turn right and follow a left-hand watercourse, later a hedge, straight on through overgrown meadows passing a bend in the river to your right and eventually turning left through a gate in the left-hand hedge and crossing a footbridge and stile. Now bear slightly right across a field to a stile by a gate in a field corner into a green lane which later widens into a small meadow and leads to a gate. Go through this and turn left following a left-hand hedge through an area of scrub to a macadam farm road. Do NOT join this road here but turn right onto bridleway SH1 making for the corner of a hedge right of a clump of tall trees. Here turn right onto the farm road, bearing left, passing a padlocked gate and crossing a bridge then after 10 yards turn right over a concealed stile onto path EY2 with Eynsham Church coming into view ahead. Now bear slightly left across the field to a stile in the next hedge then bear slightly left across a second field to another stile. Here bear slightly left again passing just right of a telegraph pole to cross a footbridge flanked by stiles in the far corner of the field. Now bear slightly left across a fourth field to a stile leading to the B4449 built on the course of the old Oxford–Witney railway.

Cross this road and a footbridge opposite into a recreation ground then turn left and follow a left-hand ditch. Where the ditch bears slightly left, turn right across the field to a corner of a hedge then follow this hedge straight on to a green gate and continue to Oxford Road. Turn left onto this road and take it (later High Street) straight on to the village centre. At a fork by the market square to your left fork right into Thames Street then at a T-junction cross the major road and turn right then immediately left onto path EY27, an alleyway called Conduit Lane signposted to the car park and toilets which leads you back to your starting point.

WALK 27:   WITNEY (SOUTH)

Length of Walk: 7.2 miles / 11.5 Km
Starting Point: Witney Town Hall.
Grid Ref: SP356096
Maps: OS Landranger Sheet 164
OS Explorer Sheet 180
OS Pathfinder Sheet 1115 (SP20/30)
Parking: There are several public car parks in central Witney.

Witney, meaning 'Witan's island', on the banks of the River Windrush at the point where it leaves the Cotswolds behind and enters the Thames Valley and where the ancient London–Gloucester road crosses the Windrush before climbing into the hills, has always formed a natural gateway to the Cotswolds. As such it is hardly surprising that it should have been here that a market developed for Cotswold Wool and a cloth-making industry became established as long as 1,000 years ago. As a result, Witney prospered, as can be seen from its magnificent thirteenth-century church with its tall spire, and by the seventeenth century was renowned for its blanket-making. Despite the industrialisation of the blanket-making industry with its attendant mills and factories and the town's considerable expansion and industrial diversification since 1945, Witney's centre with its fine old Cotswold-stone houses and civic buildings and picturesque green leading to the church has remained a place of character and interest.

The walk starts from Witney Town Hall and takes you along the town's impressive Church Green before passing former watermills, crossing the bypass and continuing through riverside meadows between the streams of the Windrush to the old centre of Ducklington with its thatched stone cottages, Norman church and village green with a pond. Having passed some of the gravel workings which now mar the lower reaches of the Windrush valley, you pass the picturesque Gill Mill before heading north through quiet countryside to skirt the scattered village of South Leigh and gently climb to the top of Cogges Hill with its panoramic views across Witney towards the Downs and Cotswolds. You then drop through Cogges passing the Manor Farm Museum and crossing the Windrush to reach Witney town centre.

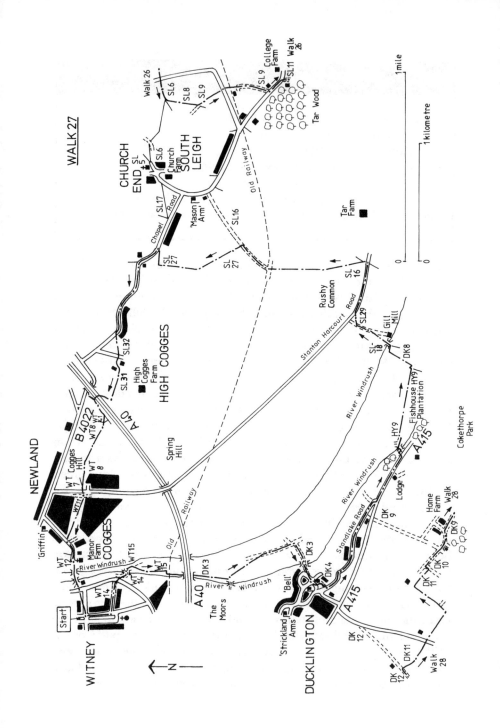

WALK 27

160

Starting from Witney Town Hall, take the road left of the seventeenth-century Butter Cross opposite towards the church passing the left side of Church Green. On nearing the church, turn left into Farm Mill Lane which soon narrows into path WT14 and continues between walls to Witan Way. Bear slightly right across this road and take macadam path WT14 right of a side road straight on through the bushes and over a bridge. Now join a road by an old mill and cross a bridge over a stream of the Windrush. At the end of the road fork right onto path WT15 following the bank of the other stream of the Windrush to gates into a field. Here fork right onto a path passing just left of some blocks of flats built on former railway sidings and crossing a raised area marking the old Oxford–Fairford railway line, this section of which opened in 1861 and closed in 1962. Now cross a stile and continue across a field to a kissing-gate by the fence of the A40 Witney Bypass.

Here pass under its river bridge (where taller walkers should duck – only 6ft headroom!) then go through a kissing-gate and take path DK3 following the river bank for some 350 yards to a kissing-gate. Now, by a large concrete bridge, bear left, still following the river bank to cross two stiles. Here bear slightly right across a field to a stile right of a willow tree with Ducklington coming into view to your right then continue to a gate and stile by the willow tree. Now follow a fenced track which eventually enters a green lane. Some 80 yards into the lane at a junction of lanes by an ash and a willow tree turn right into a lane towards Ducklington Church, eventually crossing a bridge over a stream of the Windrush and entering the village. On reaching a road called Back Lane, bear left onto it towards the much-restored twelfth-century church. By the church turn right into Church Street then immediately left past the fifteenth-century church tower to reach the edge of the picturesque village green with its large attractive pond.

Here turn left onto path DK4 beside the churchyard wall. At the far end of the churchyard turn right into a rough lane past the village hall to reach Standlake Road. Turn left onto this and follow it out of the village for over half a mile to its junction with the A415. Here ignore the entrance to Gill Mill mineral workings to your left and turn left onto the wide verge of the A415. Where the wide verge ends opposite a lodge to Cokethorpe Park, a classical house built for Sir Simon Harcourt in 1709 and now a private school, cross the road and follow its right-hand verge for a further 150 yards then turn left through a gap by overgrown gates onto bridleway HY9. Now go past a ford across one stream of the

Windrush to your left and cross a footbridge then bear left to rejoin the bridleway. Turn right onto it, soon ignoring gates to your left and following a left-hand fence to another gate. Now follow the fence and a line of white posts straight on. Where the fence turns left and the line of posts ends, go straight on across the field to a bridlegate by the left-hand end of a grass bank. Here cross a gravel road and go through a bridlegate opposite, then turn right and follow a left-hand hedge until you reach a gate in it. Turn left through this onto bridleway DK8 bearing right to the corner of a fence then left following the left-hand fence to the far side of the field. Here turn right and follow a left-hand fence to a gate in it. Turn left through this, soon crossing a bridge over the other stream of the Windrush, where the picturesque Gill Mill with its thatched weather-boarded barn comes into view to your right. Now take bridleway SL18 along a grassy track straight on past a plantation and gravel pit to join the mill drive. At the far end of the gravel pit cross a stream then turn right onto path SL29 following the stream at first then continuing across the field to a hedge gap in the far corner onto Stanton Harcourt Road.

Turn right onto this road passing a large field to your left known as Rushy Common. On nearing a right-hand bend, turn left through a gate onto bridleway SL16 crossing a culvert. Now bear slightly left ignoring a stile and footbridge to your right, joining the right-hand hedge and following it through two fields. At the far end of the second field go through a gate and cross the old Oxford–Fairford railway line then take a grassy track following a left-hand hedge to enter a wide green lane. If wishing to visit South Leigh or join Walk 26, follow this straight on to the village. Otherwise, soon after entering the green lane, turn left through a hedge gap onto path SL27 bearing slightly right across a field to a hedge gap some 50 yards left of an oak tree. Here cross a footbridge and stile and bear half left across another field to cross a stile and footbridge some 40 yards short of the first oak tree in the left-hand hedge. Now turn right and follow the right-hand hedge to the far end of the field. Here cross a footbridge and bear slightly left across the next field to a footbridge left of a clump of oak trees. Having crossed this, bear half right to gates onto Chapel Road in the top hedge left of a thatched cottage on the edge of the scattered village of South Leigh.

South Leigh Church on a rise across the fields to your right is of twelfth-century origin with a later tower and is renowned for its late mediaeval wall paintings especially that of the Soul Weighing. Its Jacobean pulpit was once used by John Wesley shortly after he nearly drowned crossing the ford at Swinford, which was superceded by the famous toll bridge in 1769.

Turn left onto this road and follow it for over half a mile. Just past a cottage with a postbox in its garden wall turn left over a stile onto path SL32 soon crossing a second stile and bearing half left across a field to cross a stile left of a cattle trough onto a road at High Cogges. Cross this road and take path SL31 straight on along a gravel drive. Where the drive forks, turn left onto a path between hedges leading to a stile into a field. Here follow the right-hand hedge straight on to the far end of the field where you turn right and follow a right-hand hedge downhill to a footbridge leading to the A40 Witney Bypass.

Cross this dual-carriageway via a staggered gap in the central-reservation crash-barrier and a stile opposite and turn left onto path WT41 following a left-hand hedge uphill. At the top end of the field disregard a stile and footbridge ahead and turn right onto path WT8 following a left-hand hedge to cross a stile by a gate. Now bear slightly right across a field on the top of Cogges Hill heading just left of a lightning-damaged treetop on the skyline with fine views to your left towards Witney Church and the distant Downs and later with panoramic views across Witney towards the Downs and Cotswolds. On reaching a stile, bear slightly left across the next field joining path WT7 and reaching a stile onto Cogges Hill Road in the far corner. Cross this road, pass through a hedge gap opposite and take macadam path WT11 straight on. At a crossways leave the macadam path and go straight on across the grass towards the right-hand end of a stone barn at the Cogges Manor Farm Museum with Witney Church coming into view to your left.

Cogges Manor Farm and the nearby parish church are virtually all that remains of the ancient village of Cogges. The church with its unusual octagonal fourteenth-century tower on a square base was originally part of a late eleventh-century priory but survived the priory's dissolution in 1414 while the thirteenth-century manor house, part of which still survives in the present buildings, replaced a nearby castle, of which earthworks can still be seen today. The mediaeval village to the south, however, has long since disappeared leaving Cogges in rural isolation until the modern expansion of Witney regrettably swamped it with a housing estate. Manor Farm, acquired by Oxfordshire County Council in 1974, is now a museum of rural life and in addition to its static exhibits offers demonstrations of rural skills and crafts.

At the far end of the green go through a gap between a stone wall and a hedge to reach a road junction by the corner of the farm buildings. Here wiggle to your right into Church Lane, the road signposted to the town centre and follow it bearing right then ignoring a branching path to your right. Soon the road narrows and becomes path WT12 crossing bridges over both streams of the Windrush. At a fork keep left to reach Witan Way by a roundabout. Cross this road and take path WT12 straight on between walls soon joining a road called Langdale Gate and following it to your starting point.

WALK 28: BAMPTON

Length of Walk: 11.9 miles / 17.7 Km
Starting Point: Bampton Market Square.
Grid Ref: SP315032
Maps: OS Landranger Sheet 164
OS Explorer Sheet 180
OS Pathfinder Sheet 1115 (SP20/30)
How to get there / Parking: Bampton, 4.7 miles southwest of Witney, may be reached from the town by taking the A4095 towards Faringdon. In Bampton there is on-street parking available, but the designated car parks should be avoided as parking there is limited to 4 hours.

Bampton, formerly called Bampton-in-the-Bush as before the construction of its first turnpike road in 1771 there was no stone-built road to the town and access to it was across a large open common, is today a picturesque old market town with numerous fine Georgian houses and cottages and a grand Town Hall built in 1838. A Saxon royal manor and the only market town in old Oxfordshire other than Oxford to be recorded in the Domesday Book, Bampton has a church of Saxon origin with a magnificent octagonal spire on a square tower with flying buttresses added in about 1270 and at one time had a twelfth-century castle of which only fragments remain. Once famous for its horse fairs and claiming to be the original home of Morris dancing, the town preserves the tradition of the annual charity Great Shirt Race when teams dressed in long gowns perform a kind of pram race round Bampton's inns to commemorate the chasing of the townspeople by Ethelred the Shirtless in 784AD in an attempt to steal their clothes.

The walk first leads you northwards from Bampton to explore the low range of hills separating the Thames and Windrush valleys with a number of fine views, visiting the hamlet of Lew with its unusual Victorian church, passing Ducklington and skirting Cokethorpe Park before dropping down to the fascinating, remote hamlet of Yelford. From here you cross the flat, but well-drained

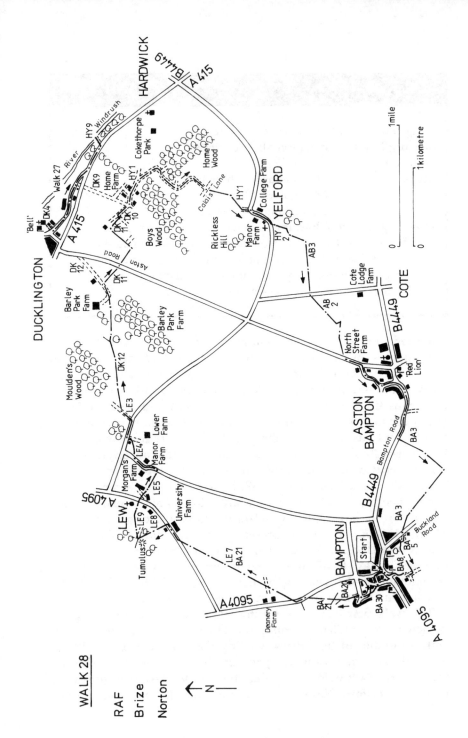

WALK 28

RAF
Brize
Norton

← N —

166

Bampton Polderland created by skilful nineteenth-century inclosure by way of Aston Bampton with its imposing Victorian church to return to Bampton.

Starting from the Market Square in the centre of Bampton, take the A4095 along Cheapside towards Witney then turn left into Church Street. At a T-junction at its far end, cross Church View and turn right onto path BA30 up a drive towards the church. Go through the churchyard gates then bear half left along a macadam path passing left of the church to reach gates onto another road. Turn left onto this then right around a sharp bend and ignore a branching path to your left. Where the road forks, bear right then immediately turn left onto path BA20, a narrow green lane leading to gates and rails into a field. Go straight on across the field to a stile left of an electricity pole then bear slightly right onto path BA21 heading just right of two cottages and a Dutch barn on the skyline to reach a gate onto the A4095, onto which you turn left.

Go round a right-hand bend then turn right through a gate onto path BA21 bearing half left across a field heading just left of a wide hedge gap on the skyline to cross a stile and footbridge in the next hedge. Now cross a track and bear half right heading for the hedge gap on the skyline, soon with views of RAF Brize Norton, established in 1937 and the largest operational RAF station, to your left and the Corallian Hills and distant Downs over your right shoulder. Go through the left side of the hedge gap then take path LE7 keeping left of a low hedge and following it to the far end of the field. Here go through a hedge gap with a functioning windpump coming into view to your right then keep straight on towards the right-hand of two copses on the skyline with more views towards RAF Brize Norton and the Cotswolds opening out to your left and towards the Corallian Hills and Downs over your right shoulder. Cross a stile in the next fence then bear half left heading right of a Nissen hut to the far corner of the field where you continue through a spinney to the A4095 on the edge of Lew.

Turn right onto this road passing University Farm. Opposite a house called Warren Close turn left over a concealed stile onto path LE8 walking parallel to a left-hand hedge to cross a stile in the far hedge. Keep straight on across the next field to a stile right of a tumulus then bear slightly right to reach a culvert in the right-hand hedge where there are fine views ahead towards the Cotswolds. Here turn right over the culvert onto path LE9 taking a fenced track for 20 yards then turn left over a stile and bear right with wide views to your left across Witney, heading for Lew Church, an Italianate structure with an octagonal tower and short spire built in 1841 by William Wilkinson, who later created the Victorian suburbs of North Oxford, and believed to be his first building. Now go through a gap in the next fence by a large elm stump then bear slightly right across the next field to a stile onto the A4095.

Cross this road and a stile opposite and, with an ancient stone cross surrounded by a ring of chestnut trees to your right, take path LE5 straight on across a paddock to a ladder stile right of a cottage. Here cross a macadam drive and continue between hedges past the end of the cottage. At the back of its garden keep straight on across wasteland to a stile then bear slightly left across a field to a stile and footbridge in the top hedge where there is a fine view of Lew House to your left. Now bear slightly left across the next field to a stile and footbridge onto a road. Turn left onto this road and follow it past Ditcham Farm, Morgans Farm and Manor Farm then just before the second large ash-tree in the left-hand hedge turn right through a hedge gap onto path LE4 bearing slightly left to pass just left of a spinney and a small pond and reach a hedge gap. Here cross a wire fence then bear half left across a field heading just right of ornamental gateposts to cross a wooden fence and join the drive to Lower Farm. Turn left onto this drive passing the gateposts to reach a road.

Turn right onto this then at a right-hand bend turn left through gates onto path LE3 along a grassy track beside a left-hand hedge. Having passed a large oak tree, look out for a gap in the left-hand hedge. Here leave the track and bear half right across a field passing left of a clump of trees and crossing a footbridge and stile right of an oak tree. Now take path DK12 bearing half right across a field to join its right-hand fence then follow it to a gate. Turn right through this then left through a second and bear half right through a clump of trees and over a rise to a gate in the next dip. Go through this and bear half right uphill to a stile by a gate in the top corner of the field. Now cross two fields diagonally aiming for a gap in trees with an electricity pole to reach a stile onto a bend in the road to Barley Park Farm.

Take this farm road straight on, soon with wide views across Witney towards Wychwood Forest to your left. About 70 yards short of some farm cottages turn right through a small gate onto path DK11 following a left-hand hedge through two fields with fine views ahead across the Thames Valley towards the Downs to reach a gate onto Aston Road. Cross this road and a stile opposite then follow a left-hand hedge across a dip to the top of the next rise. At the end of the hedge turn left passing the end of another hedge to your right and continuing towards a barn with views across Witney and Ducklington. Some 50 yards short of the barn turn right across the field walking parallel to a track to your left to reach a hedge gap. Go through this and turn left onto another track (path DK10). At a T-junction of tracks turn right to reach some barns near Home Farm. Here cross a concrete road and take a concrete road straight on, soon reverting to gravel and bearing left to reach the main farm buildings. In the farmyard fork right and take bridleway DK9 straight on out of the farm, soon becoming HY1 and entering Cokethorpe Park which has a classical house built for Sir Simon Harcourt in 1709 and now used as a private school.

In Cokethorpe Park fork right onto a gravel track beside a right-hand hedge then the edge of Boys Wood. Now continue across a field to reach Home Wood. Here follow the track bearing right along the edge of the wood, eventually passing through a gap between woods and bearing half left across a field with a fine view across the Thames Valley towards the Downs ahead. At one point the track turns sharp right to reach gates into Calais Lane. Cross this green lane, go through a gate opposite and follow a left-hand hedge to a gate at the far end of the field then bear half right across the next field to a gap by the right-hand end of the bottom hedge. Now take a green lane to a gate leading to a bend in Yelford village street.

Take this road straight on through Yelford passing the fifteenth-century timber-framed manor house of the Hastings family which later passed to William Lenthall, the celebrated Speaker of the House of Commons prior to the Civil War. On rounding a right-hand bend near the church built in about 1500 and capped by a Victorian bellcot, turn left through a hedge gap opposite the church noticeboard onto path HY2 bearing slightly right across a marshy field to a gap and culvert in the far hedge just left of an electricity pole in the next field. Go through this gap then turn right and follow the hedge. Where the hedge turns right, bear left across the field to cross a stile and footbridge just right of an oak tree and ivy-clad willow to enter the Bampton Polderland which was successfully drained by William Bryan Wood when Aston Bampton was enclosed in 1855. Now take path AB3 beside a left-hand ditch for nearly half a mile to a gate onto the Cote road. Bear half right across this road to cross a footbridge and stile virtually opposite where a fine view opens out ahead towards Aston Bampton with its early Victorian church with a spire. Now take path AB2 beside a right-hand ditch through three fields. At the far end of the third field turn left to reach a stile and footbridge then turn right over these and follow a right-hand hedge to cross two sets of rails. Here bear slightly left across the next field to a stile onto a road. Turn left onto this and follow it into Aston Bampton.

On entering the village, turn right into Back Lane and follow its winding course for over a third of a mile. At a T-junction with the B4449 (Bampton Road) turn right onto it and follow it for half a mile out of Aston Bampton. Having crossed a bridge with stone parapets, go round a right-hand bend then just past a 'Bends' sign facing the other way turn left over a footbridge and stile onto path BA3 beside a right-hand hedge. At the far end of the field continue over a culvert and through a hedge gap then bear slightly right across the next field to its far right-hand corner. Here turn right through a hedge gap and follow a left-hand stream for two-thirds of a mile ignoring a crossing farm track with a bridge at one point and continuing beside the stream until you reach Buckland Road on the edge of Bampton, a former turnpike road constructed in 1777. Turn left onto this road crossing Fisher's Bridge then turn right onto path BA5 taking a rough lane past a bungalow then wiggling right to a gate into a field. Go through this gate and follow a left-hand hedge or fence through three fields. At the far end of the third field go through a gate and turn right onto a fenced track. By Primrose Cottage ignore a ford ahead and bear half right onto enclosed gravel path BA8 which soon crosses a footbridge and continues, eventually widening into a macadam road and reaching the A4095 (Bridge Street) opposite the 'Horse Shoe Inn'. Here turn right for your starting point.

Length of Walk: 8.7 miles / 14.0 Km
Starting Point: Gates to Langford Church.
Grid Ref: SP250025
Maps: OS Landranger Sheet 163
OS Outdoor Leisure Sheet 45
OS Pathfinder Sheet 1115 (SP20/30)
How to get there / Parking: Langford, 8 miles southwest of
Witney, may be reached from the town by taking the A4095
towards Faringdon for 8 miles. Having passed through
Clanfield, turn right onto the road to Grafton, Langford and
Kelmscott. After two-thirds of a mile turn right again onto
the Grafton and Langford road. In Langford park either in the
bay opposite the church or others near the 'Bell Inn', but do
not use the pub car park without the landlord's permission.
Notes: At the time of writing path EL16 and EL33 were seriously
obstructed. If problems are encountered, alternative road
routes can be discerned from the plan.

Langford, until the nineteenth century a detached parish of
Berkshire, is a remote and attractive stone-built Cotswold-style
village in the Upper Thames plain near the Gloucestershire border.
Apart from its fine stone cottages, Langford's principal attraction
is its church, one of the few in the county of Saxon origin to
survive. Though much altered by the Normans and with aisles
added and its chancel rebuilt in the thirteenth century, the church
retains its Saxon central tower (albeit with a late Norman parapet)
and a Saxon south porch and sundial, but perhaps its greatest
treasure is the Langford Rood, a rare example of Saxon sculpture.

The walks takes you westwards from Langford by way of the
fascinating manorial village of Broughton Poggs into the quiet
foothills of the Cotswolds with their wide views to reach the idyllic
Leach valley and a Cotswold gem, the twin Gloucestershire villages of
Eastleach Martin and Eastleach Turville. You then follow the Leach
downstream past the attractive villages of Fyfield and Southrop
before re-entering Oxfordshire and turning east for Langford.

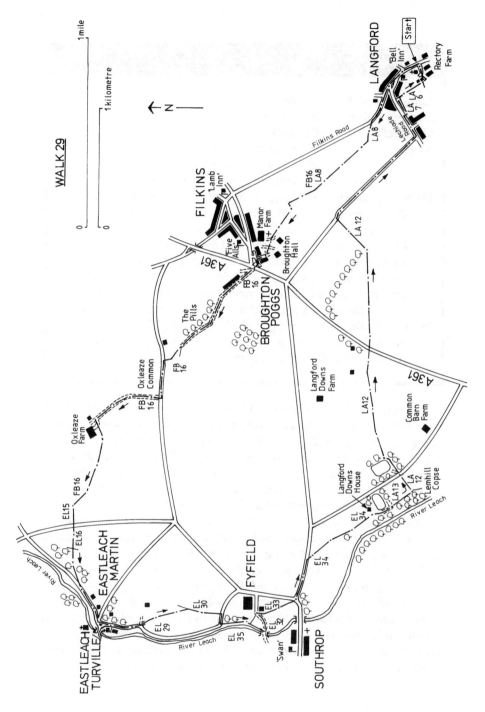

WALK 29

LANGFORD

Start

'Bell Inn'

Rectory Farm

LA 7 6

Leach Road

LA8

Filkins Road

FB16 LA8

FILKINS

'Lamb Inn'

Five Alls

Manor Farm

Broughton Hall

A361

FB 16

BROUGHTON POGGS

The Pills

FB 16

Oxleaze Common

FB 16

Oxleaze Farm

FB16

EL15

EL16

LA 12

Langford Downs Farm

LA12

A361

Common Barn Farm

Langford Downs House

LA 12

LA13

EL 34

Lemhill Copse

River Leach

EASTLEACH TURVILLE

EASTLEACH MARTIN

River Leach

EL 30

EL 29

River Leach

FYFIELD

EL 33

EL 32

EL 35

'Swan'

SOUTHROP

EL 34

N

0   1 kilometre

0   1 mile

Starting from the gates to Langford Church take the main village street northwestwards through the village passing the 'Bell Inn' and ignoring two turnings to the left and one to the right, then, soon leaving Langford. Just past the village nameboard (with its back to you) at a right-hand bend fork left through a gate onto path LA8 following a left-hand hedge straight on through three fields. In the third field, where the hedge turns left, leave it and continue across the field to cross a footbridge and stile just right of a corner of the next hedge then take path FB16 straight on beside a left-hand hedge. At the far end of the field, where Broughton Poggs Church, a solid twelfth-century building with a squat saddleback tower, comes into view ahead, go through a gate then turn left and follow a left-hand hedge to pass through another gate. Here turn right and follow a right-hand hedge to a stile into a paddock then keep straight on to cross a stile by the left-hand corner of the churchyard and join a farm track at a gate. Go through this gate then turn left through a wooden door joining a drive and following it straight on. On reaching a crossing drive where Broughton Hall can be seen to your left, go straight on through a wrought-iron gate and take a narrow enclosed path ignoring a crossing path then passing through a second wrought-iron gate. Now take a gravel drive straight on, soon reaching a village street and following it to a T-junction.

Turn left onto this road then, where the right-hand stone wall ends, turn right through a gap onto the A361. Cross this road and take a macadam drive straight on. Where the drive bears right, leave it and take bridleway FB16 straight on through four fields following a grassy track beside a right-hand hedge, later a fence, then a copse called The Pills. At the far end of the copse go straight on through a gate into another field then bear slightly left passing left of a large hawthorn bush to cross a culvert. Now continue ahead to a gate leading to a road at Oxleaze Common.

Turn left onto this road then after 350 yards turn right onto path FB16, the drive to Oxleaze Farm. At the top of a rise there are wide views to your right towards Broadwell Church, Wytham Hill, Didcot Power Station and the distant Chilterns and behind you across the Thames Valley towards the Downs. At the farm fork left onto a branching drive. Where it bears right, leave it bearing slightly left and passing through three bridlegates. Now do NOT enter a fenced ride but bear slightly right passing a corner of a fence and crossing a paddock diagonally to a horse-jump left of its far corner. Climb over this, cross a small water-jump and pass through a hedge gap then bear right across a field to a clump of tall bushes right of an ivy-clad ash-tree in the top hedge. Here go through a hedge gap and follow a left-hand hedge straight on. At a slight kink in the hedge where there is a large sarsen boundary stone buried in the hedge, turn left through a hedge gap. (BEWARE – collapsed barbed-wire fence buried in the grass!)

Now in Gloucestershire, take path EL15 bearing half right across the field heading for a thin grey metal signpost to cross a stone stile, a road and another stone stile opposite. Here take path EL16 straight on with fine views to your left towards Southrop and the Downs to reach wooden rails in the next hedge into the corner of a plantation. (In case of difficulty using this path, retrace your steps to the road then turn left and at a crossroads turn left again for Eastleach Martin.) Now go straight on, heading towards a large single oak tree on the far side of the Leach valley, entering a field and reaching a large elderbush in its bottom hedge. Here step over a barbed wire fence, descend a steep bank carefully and bear half left, dropping diagonally through a plantation with views of the Leach below you, crossing another barbed-wire fence and continuing to a stone stile in the far corner of the plantation leading to a road. Turn left onto this road and follow it to a crossroads near the church in Eastleach Martin.

The twin villages of Eastleach Martin and Eastleach Turville separated by the River Leach are two of the most picturesque villages in the Cotswolds and are unusual in that their Norman churches are a mere 150 yards apart and that, as well as the road bridge, they are connected by the only stone 'clapper bridge' in the Cotswolds. This bridge (behind Eastleach Martin Church), though reputedly ancient in origin, is known as Keble's Bridge after John Keble who was minister of both churches before going on to become a founder of the Oxford Movement and it is he after whom Keble College, Oxford (that controversial masterpiece or monstrosity of red-brick Victorian Gothic) is named. Eastleach Martin's church (the larger church in the smaller village) was built in the late eleventh century by Richard Fitzpens, who fought with William the Conqueror at the Battle of Hastings, while Eastleach Turville's church dates from the twelfth century and has a fourteenth-century tower.

At the crossroads fork left onto the Southrop and Lechlade road with fine views to your right of Eastleach Turville church and village. After 350 yards at a right-hand bend fork left onto path EL29, a stone track. Where the stone track bears left, take a sunken grassy track straight on uphill into a field then continue ahead across the field to its top hedge. Here turn right onto path EL30 following a left-hand hedge with views of Eastleach Turville behind you and later Southrop ahead. At the far end of the field go straight on through a thicket to cross a stile then continue across a field to a gate and stile onto a road. Turn right onto this road then halfway round a long right-hand bend turn left through a hedge gap onto path EL35 following the bank of the Leach for a quarter mile to reach a stone bridge over the river. Here cross a stile and turn left onto path EL32 following a stone track to a gate then across a field to a gate by a cottage at Fyfield.

Do NOT go through this gate but turn sharp right onto path EL33 following a left-hand stone wall then a fence to a corner of the field. Here climb through a loose barbed-wire fence and bear half left across a field heading for a gate in the left-hand hedge with views to your right of Southrop, in whose Norman church the young John Keble was once curate. (NB If you cannot climb through the barbed-wire fence, go back to the gate and up Fyfield village street to a T-junction then turn right to rejoin the walk at the next junction.) Go through this gate to a road junction then take the Filkins road straight on for 350 yards. At a slight right-hand bend turn right through an old gateway onto path EL34 following a right-hand hedge for nearly half a mile. At the far end of the field cross a fine old stone stile marking the county boundary and take path LA13 bearing slightly right across a paddock to enter a wide green lane right of a flooded gravel pit. At the far side of the gravel pit go straight on over a stile and across a field to join the left-hand edge of Lemhill Copse, whose name recalls the lost Gloucestershire village of Great Lemhill on the other side of the River Leach, once a detached hamlet of Oxfordshire which has now disappeared into a gravel pit.

Follow the edge of this copse to a field corner then turn left onto LA12 beside a right-hand hedge to reach a road. Cross this and take bridleway LA12 straight on through a gate onto a stone track, immediately forking right into a shady green lane passing right of a flooded gravel pit. On emerging into a field, turn right and follow a right-hand hedge through two fields. On entering a third field, bear half left across it to the corner of a hedge which you join and follow straight on to a gate onto the A361.

Cross this road and take path LA12 through a gate opposite bearing slightly left across a field to a hedge gap just right of its far left-hand corner. Go through this and turn left through a second hedge gap then bear right across a field heading just right of the far end of a line of willows to cross a footbridge and stile in the middle of the next hedge. Here bear half left to the far end of the willows joining a left-hand hedge and following it into a plantation then turn left over a concealed stile and footbridge and follow a left-hand hedge to gates onto a road. Turn right onto this road and follow it for two-thirds of a mile to the edge of Langford. At a T-junction turn left towards the village centre passing The Elms. Just before reaching a seat, turn right through a green gate onto path LA7 into a meadow then bear left across it heading for a birch and weeping willow between cottages ahead. At the far side of the field turn right onto path LA6 following back garden walls at first then bearing slightly right towards a barn at Rectory Farm with a fine view towards Badbury Forest ahead. By the barn just past a stone garage turn left over a stile and take Church Lane straight on past the church to your starting point.

WALK 30: BURFORD (SIGNET)

Length of Walk:	8.4 miles / 13.6 Km
Starting Point:	Parking area at northern end of Signet village road.
Grid Ref:	SP246104
Maps:	OS Landranger Sheet 163
	OS Outdoor Leisure Sheet 45
	OS Pathfinder Sheets 1091 (SP21/31) &
	1115 (SP20/30)

How to get there / Parking: Signet, 1 mile south of Burford, may be reached from the town by taking the A361 towards Lechlade for 1 mile. On seeing a large stone house to your right, look out for a right-hand turn signposted 'Signet only'. Here turn right then immediately right again and park where the macadam road ends.

Signet (pronounced 'sy-nit'), which apparently means 'place cleared by burning' and was not referred to till 1285, would seem from its name to have started life as a settlement in a clearing in the extensive forests which once covered western Oxfordshire. Never a large place, Signet, nestling in a protected hollow of the down-slope of the Cotswolds, now consists of a few farms and cottages just off the A361 which has been realigned to bypass the hamlet.

The walk explores the remote and generally peaceful countryside on the western edge of the county between Burford and Lechlade, where the gentle down-slope of the Cotswolds offers wide views in places across the expanse of the upper Thames Valley towards the distant Downs, visiting the tiny village of Holwell and the somewhat larger but exceptionally beautiful Cotswold village of Shilton. On occasions, however, the peace may be disturbed by aircraft noise from RAF Brize Norton and it is therefore advisable to avoid doing the walk during air shows or military exercises, etc.

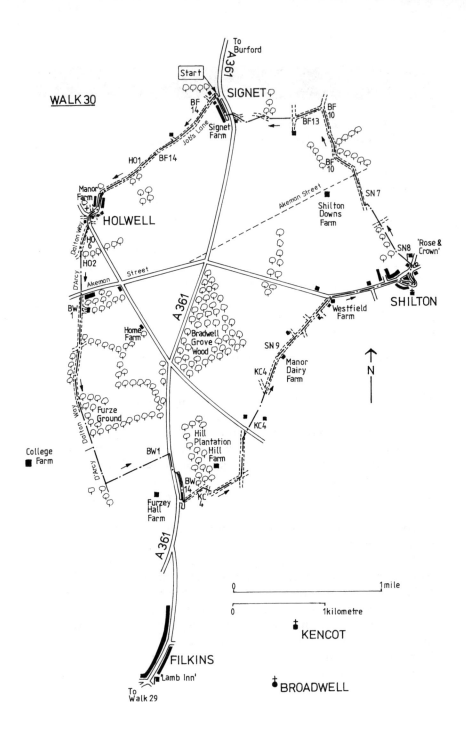

WALK 30

Start

To Burford

SIGNET

BF 14

Jobs Lane

Signet Farm

BF13

BF 10

BF 10

HO1   BF14

Manor Farm

HOLWELL

Akeman Street

Shilton Downs Farm

SN 7

Dalton Way

HO 6

HO2

Akeman   Street

D'Arcy

BW 1

SN8

'Rose & Crown'

SHILTON

Home Farm

A 361

Bradwell Grove Wood

Westfield Farm

SN 9

KC4

Manor Dairy Farm

N

Dalton Way

Furze Ground

KC4

College Farm

BW1

Hill Plantation

Hill Farm

D'Arcy

BW 14

KC 4

Furzey Hall Farm

A 361

0   1 mile

0   1 kilometre

KENCOT

FILKINS

'Lamb Inn'

To Walk 29

BROADWELL

178

Starting from the parking area at the northern end of Signet village road, take a stony lane to your left known as Job's Lane (BF14) gently downhill. Ignore two branching tracks to your right near some stables then continue over a hill for a third of a mile, soon with wide views to left and right. On reaching a gate where the main track turns right, go straight on through the gate and follow a right-hand stone wall. Near the far end of the field where the wall begins to bear right, leave it and go straight on across the field to gates in another stone wall. Here take a grassy track (HO1) gently uphill beside a left-hand hedge ignoring the first gate to your left. On nearing a belt of trees, bear slightly left through the right-hand of two gates into the end of a village street at Holwell.

Take this winding road straight on through this attractive small Cotswold village with its stone cottages with slate roofs and climbing roses. At a road junction by the Victorian village church and the war memorial fork left joining the D'Arcy Dalton Way and passing School Lodge to your right then fork right onto a fenced track (HO6). After a quarter mile in a corner of the field where the track passes through a hedge gap, leave it turning left through a gate onto bridleway HO2. Now follow a right-hand hedge past a copse and through a field to a gap in a stone wall leading to Akeman Street, a Roman road from London via Bicester to Cirencester.

Cross this road and take bridleway BW1 known as Deadman's Walk straight on along a stony lane between stone walls, later hedges, for nearly half a mile ignoring all branching tracks then after the left-hand stone wall resumes, continue until you enter a field. Here take a grassy track beside a right-hand hedge straight on, entering a green lane at the far end of the field. On emerging into another field where a fine view opens out ahead towards Coleshill and the distant Downs, follow the left-hand hedge straight on through two fields then go straight on across a third. At the far side of the third field disregard a hedge gap ahead and turn left (still on bridleway BW1 but leaving the D'Arcy Dalton Way) following a right-hand hedge through two fields to gates onto the A361.

Cross this main road and turn right onto its far verge. After about 150 yards fork left past a mound of earth onto a disused road then after a quarter mile turn left onto the crossing macadam drive to 'Minola' (bridleway BW14), soon with views to your right towards the thirteenth-century spire of Broadwell's Norman church, Coleshill and the Downs. Follow this drive gently downhill then up again (now on bridleway KC4). Some 60 yards beyond the bottom of the dip turn right through a wide hedge gap and follow the edge of a left-hand copse to pass left of an electricity pole. Now cross a concrete track and go straight on along the edge of a right-hand copse to a former runway of a wartime airfield. Turn left onto this and follow it for 350 yards with wide views to your right towards Broadwell church spire, Coleshill and the Downs. By a right-hand gate turn left onto a crossing runway and follow it for a third of a mile. Some 70 yards short of its far end bear half right off it through the bushes to a fence gap leading to the Kencot road.

Here take bridleway KC4 straight on through a fence gap opposite and across a field towards Manor Dairy Farm ahead to reach a bridlegate at the far side of the field. Go through this, then bear slightly left and take the right-hand of two fenced concrete roads straight on for three-quarters of a mile (later on bridleway SN9) passing Manor Dairy Farm and reaching a public road by Westfield Farm. Turn right onto this and follow it for half a mile ignoring the Alvescot road to your right. On entering Shilton, just past the village bus shelter and postbox and just before the manor house dating from 1678, turn right into Church Lane with its picturesque slate-roofed stone cottages with beautiful gardens. Follow its winding course for a quarter mile passing the Norman church renowned for its carved Norman font and descending to a crossroads by a ford and the attractive village green and pond.

Here cross the major road and turn right onto its footway. Opposite the village pump turn left over a stile by the gates to Byford House onto path SN8 passing left of the house then uphill between a wall and a fence to a stile into a field. Now follow a right-hand hedge straight on uphill with views of Shilton behind you to cross a stone stile then continue beside a right-hand hedge soon passing between hedges into a right-hand field where wide views open out to your right. Here follow a left-hand row of trees straight on. At the far end of the field cross a grassy track and a stone stile then keep straight on across the next field heading towards a distant barn to cross another stone stile. Now turn left and follow a left-hand stone wall to a crossing track by a gate. Here turn right onto bridleway SN7 following a wide grassy track beside a left-hand stone wall to a gate. Now take the track straight on beside a left-hand fence, later bearing left along a distinct terrace and gradually dropping into Mount Zion Bottom.

Here cross a bridge over Shill Brook, go through a gate and bear slightly left onto bridleway BF10 passing left of a clump of chestnut trees then taking a grassy track along the edge of a wood and a valley bottom. At the far end of the wood continue through a hedge gap and take a grassy track straight on beside a powerline to reach a macadam farm road. Turn left onto this road (now on path BF13) and follow it for 400 yards. Where it forks, leave it and bear slightly right across a field passing just right of a wooden electricity pole and heading for the left-hand end of a plantation ahead. Here bear half right onto a fenced track along the edge of the plantation. At the far side of the plantation turn left through gates and bear half right towards a derelict windpump. On nearing the bottom edge of the field, bear right to reach a gate right of a metal barn. Go through this then straight on to gates onto the A361 at Signet. Cross this main road and descend a steep bank right of a sycamore tree opposite to a bridge leading to the village street. Turn right onto it passing the hamlet's few cottages to reach your starting point.

INDEX OF PLACE NAMES

OXFORDSHIRE WALKS
by Nick Moon

In association with Oxford Fieldpaths Society, the two books cover walks throughout Oxfordshire to complement volume three in the same author's Chiltern Walks Trilogy.

Oxfordshire Walks 1   covers Oxford, The Cotswolds and The Cherwell Valley

Oxfordshire Walks 2   covers Oxford, The Downs and The Thames Valley

THE CHILTERN WALKS TRILOGY
by Nick Moon

These three books provide comprehensive coverage of walks throughout the whole of the Chiltern area (as defined by the Chiltern Society). Each contains thirty circular walks of varying lengths. Details of places of interest and a specially drawn map accompany each route text.

The series is published in association with the Chiltern Society, on whose behalf Nick Moon has carried out all map checking for about twenty years.

Chiltern Walks 1   covers Hertfordshire, Bedfordshire and North Buckinghamshire

Chiltern Walks 2   covers the major part of Buckinghamshire

Chiltern Walks 3   covers Oxfordshire and West Buckinghamshire

Index Map for OXFORDSHIRE WALKS book one:
OXFORD, THE COTSWOLDS and
THE CHERWELL VALLEY

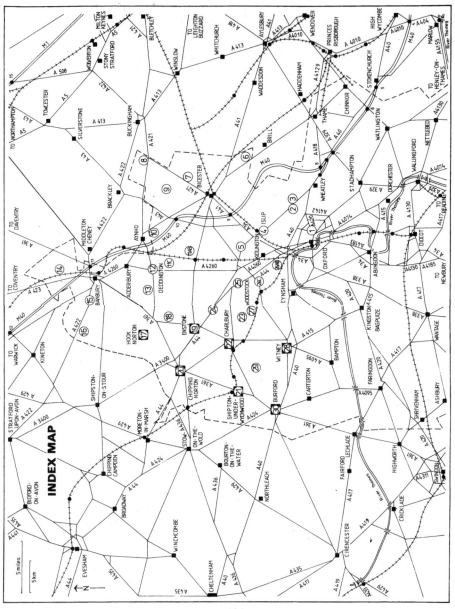

Index Map for CHILTERN WALKS book three:
OXFORDSHIRE and WEST BUCKINGHAMSHIRE

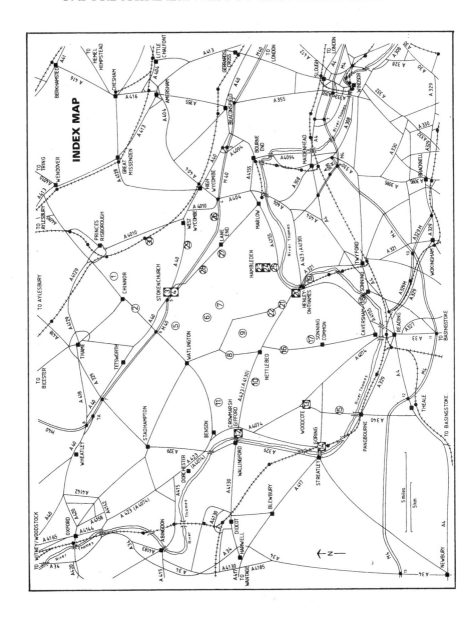

THE D'ARCY DALTON WAY
Across the Oxfordshire Cotswolds
and Thames Valley

by Nick Moon

TITLE: This guide to the D'Arcy Dalton Way; replacing the original guide written and published by the late Rowland Pomfret on behalf of the Oxford Fieldpaths Society in 1987 and now out of print, describes both the route of the D'Arcy Dalton Way itself and eight circular walks using parts of its route ranging in length from 4.0 to 13.4 miles. The text of the guide to the way and each circular walk gives details of nearby places of interest and is accompanied by specially drawn maps of the route which also indicate local pubs and a skeleton road network.
Oxfordshire County Council has kindly organised the acquisition and erection of special signposts for the D'Arcy Dalton Way.

Index Map for THE D'ARCY DALTON WAY
ACROSS THE OXFORDSHIRE COTSWOLDS
AND THAMES VALLEY

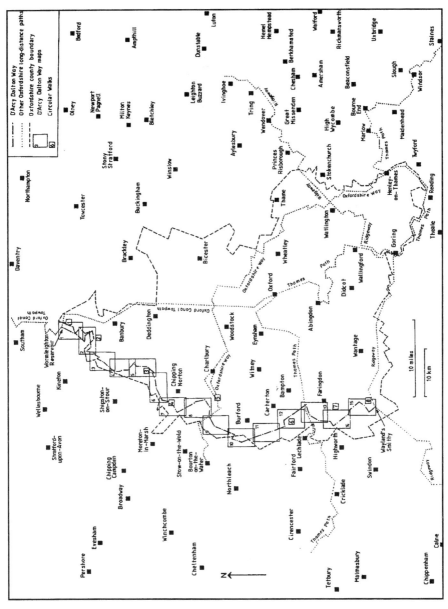

THE CHILTERN WAY

A Guide to this new 133-mile circular Long Distance Path through
Bedfordshire, Buckinghamshire, Hertfordshire & Oxfordshire

by Nick Moon

The Chiltern Way has been established by the Chiltern Society to mark the
Millennium by providing walkers in the twenty-first century with a new
way of exploring the diverse, beautiful countryside which all four Chiltern
counties have to offer. Based on the idea of the late Jimmy Parsons' Chiltern
Hundred but expanded to cover the whole Chilterns, the route has been
designed by the author and is being signposted, waymarked and improved
by the Society's Rights of Way Group in preparation for the Way's formal
launch in October 2000. In addition to a description of the route and points
of interest along the way, this guide includes 29 specially drawn maps of the
route indicating local pubs, car parks, railway stations and a skeleton road
network and details are provided of the Ordnance Survey and Chiltern
Society maps covering the route.

Index Map for THE CHILTERN WAY
A 200KM CIRCULAR WALK ROUND THE CHILTERNS

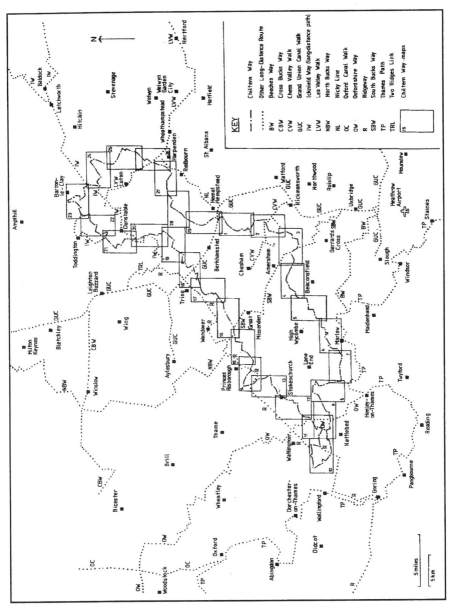

FAMILY WALKS
Chilterns - South

FAMILY WALKS
Chilterns - North

by Nick Moon

A series of two books, which provide a comprehensive coverage of walks throughout the whole of the Chiltern area. The walks included vary in length from 1.7 to 5.5 miles, but are mainly in the 3 to 5 mile range, which is ideal for families with children, less experienced walkers or short winter afternoons. Each walk text gives details of nearby places of interest and is accompanied by a specially drawn map of the route, which also indicates local pubs and a skeleton road network. The author, Nick Moon, has lived in or regularly visited the Chilterns all his life and has for 25 years, been an active member of the Chiltern Society's Rights of Way Group, which seeks to protect and improve the area' s footpath and bridleway network.